MINING FOR STARDUST

FLOWERSONG
P R E S S

MINING FOR STARDUST
Copyright © 2021 by Kai Coggin

ISBN: 978-1-953447-45-6
Library of Congress Control Number: 2021947500

Published November 2021 by FlowerSong Press
Printed in the United States of America
www.flowersongpress.com

Cover design by Joann Saraydarian & Kai Coggin

Cover image origin: NASA Hubble Telescope image of Pillars of
Creation in the heart of the Eagle Nebula. Image by NASA and the
Space Telescope Science Institute (STScI). No claim to copyright is being
asserted by STScI and material may be freely used as in the public domain
in accordance with NASA's contract.

Author photo by David Yerby

FlowerSong Press
1218 N. 15th St.
McAllen, Texas 78501

info@flowersongpress.com

MINING FOR STARDUST

POEMS

KAI COGGIN

ADVANCE PRAISE

"In *Mining for Stardust*, a chronicle that salvages life from a year of deadly pandemic, the poet lays her words down at 'the holy feet' of her wife, and praises the sacred earthy gifts of fat frogs, red-bud blossoms, the 'sun-bleached bones' of a fox 'vertebrae articulating/something I haven't the words for yet.' She grieves and praises 'the African dust...calling to her stolen children...the great gardener tilling the soil'--and grieves and praises the fallible humans, us in our 'islands of want' that we turn into graveyards for burying, that we turn into gardens for planting. Jubilantly, she claims the queer beauty of the world, the Milky Way all 'shimmer and shine' like fireflies-- 'bioluminescent beings seeing each other.' She says to us, 'It shines, darling—it shines for you.'"

— **Minnie Bruce Pratt**,
author of *Magnified*

"Kai Coggin's *Mining for Stardust* is filled with love poems—to her wife and the life they have made together, as well as to the natural world in which they're both so immersed. This new collection reads as a kind of heartfelt journal of the first pandemic year, yet each of these wide-sweeping poems reaches far past current events, toward the more universal truth of 'what stitches us together.' Kai Coggin is a necessary voice who knows how to praise this difficult world even as her poems call for social justice and equality, urging us all to 'let what truly matters matter more than ever.'"

— **James Crews,**
editor of *The Path to Kindness: Poems of Connection and Joy*

"Kai Coggin embraces Mother Nature holistically, reverently, ecstatically. Holistic poetry sees the connection between all living things, the world, the universe. Reverent poetry pays attention and gives praise. Ecstatic poetry sings life and death into being in words. But Coggin's lesbian love poems are the most wonderfully moving for me, since they bring all of the above, plus two women together in nature. *Mining for Stardust* is a kind of cosmic healing our world desperately needs."

— **Mary Meriam**,
author of *My Girl's Green Jacket*

"Kai Coggin's fourth poetry book, *Mining for Stardust*, is a stunning and timely collection beginning at the start of the pandemic lockdown and taking the reader on an inspirational journey. Her opening poem centers the book in love; she asks 'Who are you spending the end of the world with tonight? / Do yourself a favor and hold them tight.' Throughout this collection, vivid images capture our collective fears and our hopes, while always inspiring us to move forward. Coggin's spectacular poems are a guidepost for these challenging times. She gifts us love in multiple forms, including love of her wife, love of community, and love of nature; love is the stardust connecting these poems. When Coggin tells us 'we are all just searching out truth and tenderness, / some light to cling to in this darkness, / a feeling that we are still somehow connected' her words are a balm, a light, a ray of hope during these unprecedented times."

— **JP Howard**,
author of *SAY/MIRROR*

"Beautiful, lyrical, expansive, and sprawling, Kai Coggin's *Mining for Stardust* is poem as prayer, poem as embrace. Navigating her way through the difficult political and personal times of our global pandemic, Coggin plants beauty everywhere, from her yard to her heart garden to the word garden that is this book. Page after page, poem after poem, I was broken open until I too was filled with hope and brightness, until I too was a planet, a wildflower, 'light written in stars on a mountaintop.' Mining for Stardust is a place where the moon and heart are always full, and where the tenderness and passion of newlywed bliss ignites everything. Finishing this book, I wanted two things: to re-read it immediately and to gift it to everyone I encountered. For, if everyone were to see how beautiful it can be to live wide-open, as a conduit of love in all its forms and gestures, then I can't help but feel that the whole world would change."

— **Melissa Studdard**,
author of *I Ate the Cosmos for Breakfast*

ABOUT PILLARS OF CREATION COVER IMAGE:

These towering tendrils of cosmic dust and gas sit at the heart of M16, or the Eagle Nebula. The aptly named Pillars of Creation, featured in this stunning Hubble image, are part of an active star-forming region within the nebula and hide newborn stars in their wispy columns.

Although this is not *Hubble's* first image of this iconic feature of the Eagle Nebula, it is the most detailed. The blue colors in the image represent oxygen, red is sulfur, and green represents both nitrogen and hydrogen. The pillars are bathed in the scorching ultraviolet light from a cluster of young stars located just outside the frame. The winds from these stars are slowly eroding the towers of gas and dust.

Stretching roughly 4 to 5 light-years, the Pillars of Creation are a fascinating but relatively small feature of the entire Eagle Nebula, which spans 70 by 55 light-years. The nebula, discovered in 1745 by the Swiss astronomer Jean-Philippe Loys de Chéseaux, is located 7,000 light-years from Earth in the constellation Serpens. With an apparent magnitude of 6, the Eagle Nebula can be spotted through a small telescope and is best viewed during July. A large telescope and optimal viewing conditions are necessary to resolve the Pillars of Creation.

Credits: NASA, ESA and the Hubble Heritage Team (STScI/AURA)

Source: https://www.nasa.gov/image-feature/the-pillars-of-creation

FOR JOANN

my wife & north star

AND FOR THE 4.4+ MILLION SOULS LOST IN THE PANDEMIC

TABLE OF CONTENTS

"Pick a flower on Earth
and you move the farthest star."

— **Paul Adrien Maurice Dirac**, Quantum Physicist

"There's as many atoms
in a single molecule of your DNA
as there are stars in the typical galaxy.
We are, each of us, a little universe."

— **Neil deGrasse Tyson**, *Cosmos*

⌘ A Poet's Balcony Aria in the Apocalypse

Through my headphones,
I listen to a quarantined Italian tenor
balcony-serenade the empty streets and rooftops of Florence,
I listen as his climax permeates the sky like an arrow into my heart,
Nessun Dorma— none shall sleep,
eyes are finally opening to our own collective frailty.

I play the aria again for my love,
and we watch the strength
of the air pulled into the tenor's chest,
the breath released with the high B *Vincerò!*
as he clutches the balcony railing
bursting at the seams with feeling
for his country,
for his people
on their solitary balconies,
he picks his little son up into his arms
as if to say we will survive this
and sky-sings another *Vincerò!— 'I will be victorious'*

My wife and I weep for the beauty
(I call her my wife in this poem
because there is no one else
I would rather spend the end of the world with)
and without saying it, we weep for this tragedy as well.

She goes about filling the first hummingbird feeder of the season
and I write this poem with an aria in my throat
and this blank page balcony
hoping the words will come,
something with meaning through the meaning-lost time.

What shall we sing from our balconies and fire-escapes
as we walk day by day into this unfolding apocalypse?

1

What will we gravitate to in the dark?
What matters most to you when tomorrow is no longer yours?

My Facebook feed is fearful and frenetic,
oversharing of resources and lessons and links
as we desperately try to connect and hold onto to one another,
like we are all throwing each other life-rafts
but our country is a sinking ship
and the ocean is already in our lungs.

My love comes in from outside,
she collects bright apples from the bowl
and peels them to make a pie,
the sun has finally started to shine after ten solid days of rain,
the cardinals and bluebirds outside trade arias of their own.

I tell her wild boar are running the vacant streets of Italy,
the swans and dolphins again swim the canals in Venice,
the water is so clear schools of fish can be seen to the bottom
and the people have no living memory of ever seeing this before—
eyes are finally opening to Earth's human-less harmony.

She tells me the air pollution over China has almost disappeared,
satellites in space are noticing the clarity of our skies,
and I think of what the earth must be feeling through this,
what deep breath she must be taking as we are holed away inside.

I wonder what few American wonders will flourish
if we all heed the calls for quarantine
and quiet our capitalism for a few months
to let nature reconvene.

Will the subway trains whirr a song of ghosts?
Will the Grand Canyon become an exhale?
Will our rivers and streams remember their dreams?
Will wildflowers run for Congress?
Will our mountains remind us how to stand up for each other?
Will decency bloom through the untrodden sidewalk cracks of our cities?
Will this finally remind us of our collective humanity?

Be still.
Be quiet.
Be solitary and slow.
Be attentive and listen.

In a couple of weeks, we will wear Italian shoes—
they walked this unknown first and we surely will follow
in our losses, in our fears, and in our hopes that we will survive this,
our collective American bravado will be cut down at the knees,
and millions will wish they had only listened to the pleas
to stay inside,
to be alone
together.

I wonder in the weeks to come, what will return to our land?
What new suns will rise over our beaten fields?
Let the crops grow wild with no one to tend them. Let the birds own the
spring again with their nesting and song.
Let us humans acknowledge all we have done wrong.

Let the children feel their parents closer
and slowed down
and present,
learning lessons like communicating expression,
or shaving with dad, or tying a tie,
or collecting all the apples together and baking a pie.

Let the parents slow down
and remember the wonders of imagination,
and take their children on indoor adventures of the heart.
This is the most important way you can do your part.

Let the walls be broken down and the uniting bridges stand tall.
There is no real separation, when the danger comes for us all.

Let the cloud we didn't even know we were living in, lift.
Let what truly matters matter more than ever— maybe that is the gift.

Who are you spending the end of the world with tonight?
Do yourself a favor and hold them tight.

⌘ I Wanted to Believe

I wanted to believe
that the dolphins had really returned
to the clearwater canals in Venice,
the swans too—
their feathers gleaming
in the human-less sunshine.
I wanted to believe
in the playful elephants
passed out in a tea garden in China,
gleefully drunk on corn wine.

I was quick to share
the feel good feelings,
the hope,
the natural world's resurgence
that we all wanted to believe was happening,
to find greater purpose
in this uncertain time of unprecedented distance,
like a divine architecture had stepped in to rebalance the scales,
and so I joined with millions of others
in the viral spread
of news
and now learning that it was all untrue
brings me into a different sort of stillness.

It's the ninth day of quarantine
and I can hear the birds singing in the morning,
but that's how we always wake up,
with the birds singing,
with the scurry of chipmunks
hoovering sunflower seeds off the back deck,
with a family of deer grazing on the green lawn below—
the daily balance
of human and animal life we cultivate
right here at home.

Still, the stillness. The silence.

It's the ninth day of quarantine
and though the western world
is indefinitely sequestered,
or at least should be,
spring is still unfurling
all her glorious colors,
outside, the leaves are breaking
open from buds reaching sky,
and I was so stunned by the raindrops
that lingered on the petals of a small wood violet
that I picked it gently and brought it inside.

It's the ninth day of quarantine
and I literally spent half an hour
taking professional photos of fat frogs
sitting on hot stones around our koi pond,
the sun making their frog skin reflect a bronze light,
seven frogs in some kind of koi pond conference—
what do they know that they aren't telling me?

It's the ninth day of quarantine,
and I am looking at everything
a little closer these days,
zooming in more on the natural world
as it tilts from one season into another,
and I found a small bird's nest
precariously snugged into the branches of a short sapling,
pine needles and dried brown oak leaves in a tight circle
woven with a mastery that had withstood the battering
rains of the past few weeks—
god, I hope we can hold it together as well as this.

I wanted to believe
that the dolphins had returned
to the clearwater canals in Venice,
the swans too—

and even though that is not true,
my friends are posting more pictures of sunsets
and wildflowers they find on their solitary forest hikes,
and the frogs and koi and bluebirds and spring
are singing just outside my door in a language
I am hearing so much clearer now,
and we are all just searching out truth and tenderness,
some light to cling to in this darkness,
a feeling that we are still somehow connected
in our isolated worlds, waiting,
mining stories of hope so we can cope,
and yes we are using Zoom to connect with our former selves,
but we are also zooming in on what really matters
when all else goes out of focus,
like a bokeh to the broken systems we once thought were real,
and tell me—

when you zoom in, what does your world reveal?

⌘ Mourning Song Two Weeks into the Pandemic

it's the morning
of the first day of
national poetry month
and all I can hear
this morning is mourning

mourning poetry month
national mourning month
national poetry mourning

it slips into every line
moves stark against words
this unsettling reality settling in
in every sound this morning
this mourning

of all we do not yet know
of all that we have lost

five thousand today
or is it five million

and all of my pages
are white flags
at half-mast
this
morning

⌘ Planting Seeds and Tasting Flowers During the End of Days

we plant seeds in the rain today
a slow drizzle falling on our faces
as we bend over the little herb garden bed

we share a pair of green knee pads
both wearing one on our right leg like
the uniform of some rogue gardening gang

the rain beads on our slick jackets
as we sprinkle arugula spinach basil
thyme and I cannot help but think

of the ancient line about the wise man
planting a tree under whose shade he will never sit
and in these days of darkness and death

is this simple act of planting seeds an act of survival—
I pull myself from that thread of thought
and come back to the rain falling gently

the cool breeze and my gloveless hands
how I want to feel the dirt cake my palms in meaning
I want to feel the earth merge with my skin

want to take in this cycle of birth and blooming
I plant my palm-full of seeds and shuffle the soil gently
with my fingers like a spell of hope cast in the grains of terra

we plant red star and white cypress vines for the hummingbirds
and I can already see them climbing and swirling the stone wall and bamboo
spilling over like a watercolor

I go inside and pour us each a shot of soft rose liqueur
in the handprinted geisha glasses I got in Japan
we swirl our wrists like climbing vines and taste flowers

I've learned when you *cheers* with someone
you always look the other person in the eyes
her eyes are so blue out here like a new day against the grey

I kiss her and the rain kisses our cheeks
and kisses the newly buried soon-to-be herbs
and our first seed planting phase is done

sun— phase two up in the new bamboo walled garden
is a little more technical less willy nilly— serious
she has mapped out an intricate color-coded seed distribution model

studied the antagonists of beets and russian pickling cucumber
charted out the friendliest neighbors for dragon carrots and radish
and we make the map to scale with our hands and hearts in the dirt

she handles the climbers trellis-training them even as embryo
the snow peas the empress and sultan green crescent beans
and who knew that these tiny things could be so majestically named

what if we all knew our majesty at such an early stage
what if we all knew before rooting who we would flourish next to
and who would leave us broken— garden philosophy

I plunge my finger into the soil in precise but artistic regions
following of course the meticulous color mapping
and drop the little dreams of harvest into their respective holes

the prize bok choy and black beauty zucchini
the long cucumbers rainbow chard and celery
and I have never planted seeds like this in a garden like this

and I will just add this to the infinite list of moments of beauty
she creates and cultivates with me
and we smile at each other as we push these little hopes into the earth

as she finishes up I pick a handful of bright red-bud blossoms
and cup them in my soil-caked hand the colors so profoundly pink
we share their succulence and sour literally tasting flowers

we water all that we have laid into the the ground
hope for their breaking open and reaching for the sun
knowing this year we will not go hungry whatever may come

⌘ Lazarus

it's palm sunday
a moveable feast
that has been moved
inside
minus   the palms
minus   the hands
minus   the peace

and I speak only in these fragmented psalms
but my palms ache to touch you

bring my fingers to bless your cheekbones
sweep your eyes with supple thumbs
cradle your neck and pull you
into me

our passion play
I lay myself down at your holy feet—
bend my fronds under your weight
lazarus me with your kiss

the lines of my hands
shape words into worlds
that want to blend with yours
fortune tell a sense of longing and loss
and we are islands of want

around the world
palms are empty
in waiting
in desperation
in quiet prayered plea

we scrub and scrub
soaping the hope

we will not become casualty
and lately this theme pervades all my poetry
these hours days weeks months in solitary

⌘ Today I Washed My Hands in a Mucky Koi Pond

Today I washed my hands in a mucky koi pond
and I never felt more clean,
I did not scrub or scald
my palms and wrists and fingers,
no song lingered in my head
telling me when to quit scrubbing,
no bubbles or suds
only silt and mud
and the water was freezing.

Call me thrill-seeker
but the five koi fish needed a bath,
the falling of leaves and the winter's freeze
were both politely asked if they could leave
because my darling and I had sunshine
a pump a hose and a plan
and today I washed my hands
where parrot-feathers green sprawling algae vines
intertwined with mine.

Call me brazen
but I changed my jeans into cutoff shorts
my work boots into river shoes
and became a slick fish
Koi Kai
and Peneloped myself into the pond
but I didn't go there to die,
I walked in to resurrect spring in the water
usher my underwater friends into a new season,
slow and cautionary
my ankles and shins froze,
as my fin(ger)s dove down to the leaves
blanketing black the pond bottom,
my hands became wet rakes
grabbing and slopping decaying autumn to shore,

my beloved (wo)manned the pump,
siphoned half the chilly water out and over the lip to dry land,
and today I washed my hands between slippery bright orange fish,
calling them each by name
Rocket - Luna - Goldie - Pinx - Biggie Stardust.

Call me childish
but with each scoop of leaves I begged to touch them,
for them to swim up to me like little dogs
but not being able to clearly see through the water,
I jumped back and squealed when
my rake-hands slowly brushed their fish bodies,
we laughed and I smiled wide like a child,
and this type of innocence
is not for most people,
this type of shared tenderness
but today I washed my hands and my feet and my legs
like a little girl splashing and giggling in a muddy puddle.

Call me sentimental
but I get attached,
and when I name something it becomes mine,
my children of other kingdoms,
and the all white koi who came to me in a dream
I named Rice Paper,
he vanished in the fall and I thought he was just hiding,
all this time tucked away
because he was just too beautiful
to be bothered by all this winter,
and every day as the weather started warming
I would do a little head count
wishing to find his beautiful white tail
paintbrushing sky reflections
1 2 3 4 5
never 6
and today I washed my hands with a ghost.

I remember us digging this giant hole,
laying the liner

and dragging these stones and boulders
to edge this hope of a new world,
and how we filled it with fresh water
and lilies and dreams that one day in the future
we would sit at our koi pond
and silently watch the fish swimming
in infinite patterns of color just under the surface,
and today
the world outside is a different world,
the paradigm of everything we know
is shifting like a rockslide
into a chasm of what we do not know—
but we *do* know that our koi fish are strong,
the yellow irises on the shore are sprouting mighty and rooted,
a chorus of huge frogs conferences daily on the hot stones,
dragonflies dance an aerial ballet,
and their friendly pond is clean,
empty of leaves and muck,
filled with fresh water and joy
and today I washed my hands in it
over and over again.

⌘ Into Wildflower Into Field

it's dusk and I watch you
water our newly-planted garden
the radish and arugula
are first to push up through the soil
green hands in prayer
unfolding toward sun and sky
and I sit on the side and write
as you coax them
toward you

it's like you're singing
invisibly to the sleeping bed of seeds
like I can see the vibration of
your gentle harvest hope

my own fingers
begin searching the earth
my body bends toward the light
of you
I green into a personal spring
my seeds
break open again
and again
searching for sun and sky *(your eyes)*

constant gardener—
you water the drought of me
into wildflower
into royal meadow
into fields and fields and fields

did you ever think our lives
would bloom into this?

on the ridge-line
the setting day paints
us in an impermanent gold
but even now in the darkest dark of night
everything around us is aglow

⌘ Temple Dogs 石獅賦

(for Genghis & Layla, Fu Dogs)

If my heart is the temple,
let them always stand as guardians,
small lions,
Fu-fierce-fur-balls
that stand parallel pi squared,
chest out proud little boxes,
earth and mankind under their paws,
coming from the star trails of comets,
or Sirius, the dog star,
or the tip of the Great Bear's nose,
or just some sweeter dimension than here.

I recognize the ancient blessing they are,
little pekingese,
little peeking eyes
in the consciousness of my lifetimes,
they walked the lifelines
back to me on the leash of goodness and love.

I have renamed
the chambers of my heart Genghis & Layla,
yin and yang, him and her,
both equal in strength, in softness,
in ferocity and fur.

There is a magic carpet
that takes me in my dreams
and they are the flight and levitation,
the elevation that ensues the moment we snooze,
the wonder
snoring beside me,
their little tufts of breath
make a song that unshackles

the earthly body
and opens up the spirit to swirl around the cosmos,
yes, these little dogs do that,
these little walking forces of beauty and protection,
these four-legged masters.

The emperors of ancient Peking
            the forbidden city
carried pocket size pekingese in the hammocks
of their crimson silk robe sleeves,
they would inspect emperor's cuisine
and bark of poisons,
they would snap at the ankles
of those who breached the walls,
they would guide the leaders of dynasties
to use their intuition and hearts,
sleeve pekingese,
oh please never leave pekingese,
tiny emissaries on a mission
of protection,
and I am no forbidden city empress,
but these small lions,
one black,
one white,
these two giants,
these fuzzy angels,
these small soft ninjas
are my eyes in the sky,
the warrior guardians of my soul.

In the mornings,
they are warm bundles,
contoured
around
            my contours,
shaping
            what
                        love
            feels
like.

Genghis & Layla,
Heart Temple Fu Dogs,
I found out when writing this poem
赋 (fu) means poetry in Chinese,
see what I mean about the gifts they bring—
my spirit animals,
my animal spirits,
two sides
of the coin that I am,
the sweet and the fierce,
the licks of love
and punctures of bite,
the black and the white,
they mingle and mix and reflect ALL,
divine little mirrors,
my tufted wings,
flying me higher and higher
to
the temple
within my Self.

⌘ The Fox Comments on Proper Burial Procedure at 10,000 Dead

I rake a path
through the woods,
change the energy of the land,
move leaves and earth with
the sweep of my hands,
layers of seasons
crunchy brown,
the wet year before
yellow decaying
until I hit pure ground,
dark dirt.

Winding and curving
the soft wet forest in silence,
one rake uncovers
the sun-bleached bones of a quick fox,
years white fade blaring bone bright
against the mud-colored floor.

I see the shape of him
the movement
the grace
of his fossilized grandeur,
his delicate hind leg,
maybe a shoulder
blading through the grass,
vertebrae articulating
something I haven't the words for yet.

I pick up a tiny white backbone,
hold its weightlessness in my palm,
turn it in my fingers
against the glint of fading day
and I remember the headlines

out of New York City this morning—
"contingency plan"
"ten coffins for each trench"
"NY city park"

the words *"dignity"* and *"only temporary"*
flash in my eyes
as light bounces off bone
and there is nowhere to bury all the bodies.

There is nowhere to bury all the bodies.
I think of the American shut-ins
balcony-howling in unison each night into the open sky
to thank the essential workers,
beating their pots and pans and hands
together like the tribe vibration is returning to them,
the thread is thicker than the threat
that connects us all.

My heart sets itself on fire
and I howl,
I scream so loudly the birds
explode from the trees
and the mountain sings back to me.

AoooOOOOOOOOOOO

I lay the fox vertebrae
back in line with the fox spine,
leave him as whole as I found him
and cover his bones with the pure black earth.

I hope
our 10,000 dead countrymen
receive the same dignity
wholeness
rest

⌘ Lately My Friends Have Been Giants

lately, my friends have been giants
white oak pine silver maple sweet gum
hovering tall overhead
with their crown shyness,
letting just enough sun in
to reach down to me

I talked to a yellow tiger swallowtail
for twenty minutes
as he danced nectar-drunk
on the purple verbena blooms,
we traded recipes—
he gave me a cup of flowers

I watched a chipmunk stuff his cheeks
with as many sunflower seeds as he could,
bringing them back to his elaborate tunnel system,
and I imagine a catacomb of sunflowers blooming
under our orchard of fruit trees

my morning meditation
is skimming the tree-sex
off the surface of the koi pond,
wind pollinating water
and catkin falling
like a million flying brown worms
onto the glassy mirror
smudged with spring—

with every hand sweep of the pond skimmer
I visualize the earth getting swept clean,
the haze being crystal clear
and that all of us
come through this
into a new clarity of compassion

I whistle *somewhere over the rainbow*
and I sneeze
from the sex
of hundreds of millions of trees

⌘ Too Wide To Bridge

it's good friday,
the middle of the night
and I try to sleep but can't
quiet the mind spinning
in so many directions at once,

it's good friday
and it was good, honestly,
and I didn't even know
the day of the week until I laid down,
spent hours photographing
chipmunks and bluebirds and butterflies
in the spring-bursting sun,

.

while outside these paradise walls
a covid crucifixion is
hammering nails into boxes holding
thousands of my brothers
and thousands of my sisters,

and tonight
there are prisoners
in hazmat suits
getting paid $6/hr
digging New York mass graves
stacking up pine caskets of the unclaimed,

these are the ones that nobody comes for,
the ones who die alone,
the ones who have no friends or family,
no kids of their own,

and I don't know how to sit with this—
this chasm is too wide to bridge
with a poem,

25

but it's good friday
and no, no it was not good,
and I just had to write that into the gospel of now.

⌘ A Baptism Reflecting the Celestial

It's the full moon pink and super
in the middle of the day
and we walk in our woods
for the first time together in five months,
your fragile body remembering itself after tasting death twice,
regenerating after the last painful surgery,
(I can't believe I almost lost you before all this, my love,
how you beat death only to have it thrust onto the whole planet at once,
how time is a force that reckons with us, and you are still here).

We are careful and brave.

It's the full moon and the path we share
with the family of deer who sleep here is filled with bright ferns,
the speckled sunlight from felled trees has changed
the landscape to druid fairy wonder
sprout-shouting green at our feet,
unspeakable neon beauty.

The dogs flank us ahead and to the rear,
I walk close behind you,
watch your steps,
hold the air at your back
as you charge forward to the stream,
(I would follow you anywhere, love).

We check the integrity of the pine bridge
we built a couple of years ago,
sturdy but needing care *(like us both)*
and water rushes underneath
cutting through forest to our lake.

We wind the path through a study in moss
and I almost disappear into a tiny world,
microcosm myself into a mushroom's underbelly,

until your voice calls from the lake edge
(you, my constant heart compass).

Our water is milky jade turquoise blue after the rains—
I have never seen color like this.

Genghis is already paws in the shallows,
mingling with tadpoles and panting a song,
I go in ankle deep and it's freezing,
the slow thaw of this body
of water
takes weeks into summer to be swimmable
but this is a day that calls for daring
and I strip off my clothes
and you ask

> *are you really going in?*

I know I don't *want* to dive into this icy jade
but you need a jolt
and I need you to know
that I would icefish naked for minnows
for you to baptize this day anew,
for your body to come back to me reborn,
for your soul to remember its light,
and suddenly
your clothes are off, too.

You step into the indescribable color
and turn around to face me,
your eyes are the exact same shade as the pulsing lake,
infinite ripples appear to emanate out from your head
and I am utterly transfixed by you.

How can someone fall so many times in love?
Every cell of me opens.

> *There is nothing to do but just do it!*

you say and you turn and dive like a swan or a star
or a swan-star-moonbeam
and oh yeah— the moon is full right now,
at this very moment in the middle of the day
and you, my love, are body baptized in a fresh spring.

I do the it's-so-cold dance at the edge
until counting to three and diving in,
rush cold freeze punch of waking,
our hearts crack wide and we swim back to earth,
a hawk circles overhead and I swear I hear him cheering.

It's the full moon right now,
and you pull out your pocket planet app,
and point your iPhone right above us,
the Sun transiting Pisces—
your birth sign,
and us, two cold little fish.
Where is the moon right now?

I ask and you point
searching until you find it under your feet,
glowing full ball of light in Virgo,
your rising sign,
a sign you're rising,
mother constellation,
Virgin
birthing
Christ full moon from her celestial body,
water birth baptism in our lake, directly underfoot a reflection
on the other side of the planet at this exact moment—
as above so below and how does one measure such synchronicities
except with the infinite?

We are not religious women,
but there is something holy about diving naked into freezing waters,
something holy about coming back to your body,
jolting away the trauma like a sword unsheathing,
and you have always forged yourself

in fire
in water
in earth
and you glint before me with a new radiance, alive.

You, and the brightest full moon in the middle of the day.

⌘ Essence

I thinned the seeds already sprouting
in the bamboo garden
the radish beet carrot and bean

pulled each birth
out of the earth
and laid it on my tongue
crushed it with my teeth

and did you know these tiny sprouts
these little leaves and baby greens
already hold the heavy flavors of their final selves?

if only we tasted our own essence from birth
knew the transformations to come
were all part of the becoming—

that we had the imprint all along.

⌘ Fertile

I have so much
dirt
under my fingernails
from gardening

so much thick soil
new mooning black
I could plant ten thousand seeds
in these garden (nail)beds
and sprout a whole forest of trees

make a whole ecosystem
under my touch
huddle
the howling fox
the heavy elephant
the sky-kissing giraffe
the wild black bear
and quick cheetah
to rest quiet in my palms

perch the screech owl
the eagle
and the wide-wing condor
between my fingers

lifelines turned riverbed
fresh with moving water for all who thirst

because I have so much
of the earth
under my fingernails
coated
on my hands

I swear that
my whole body is fertile
for planting

⌘ Tendrils

I seem to be finding
all of my poems
in the garden,

this isolation from people
has me speaking
in the language of leaves

and leaving, this morning
I find my poem in the raveling snow peas,
twisted up in their reaching

their climb and striving up
the guiding trellis all tendrils and swirl
all growing and beauty unfurling

more and more each moment,
the way I reach for you
more and more each moment,

all wanting and ache unfurling
the way my gentle tendrils reach and ravel
into the
space

between us.

⌘ Baby Blues

It's easter morning
and a storm blew in last night
that underwatered our everythings—

I jolt awake to peek at the careful nest
of pine needles the returning bluebird couple
built in the corner rain gutter outside
our bedroom window,
I had been leery of their real-estate choice
rainwashing away
when I first saw papa bluebird
fly back and forth from the corner perch
in the first suns of spring,
but dismissed my human worry
because these birds must know
what they are doing,
wouldn't risk
the four bright blue eggs
who patiently sat in the circle
of tightly woven warmth.

I have spent days excited
to watch the season of hatching,
to hear the baby blues crying for worms
and see them fumbling toward flight.

I have already been writing
the poems in my head,
the sequel of miracles that this family
brought back to our house,
writing the rituals of their blue blue love.

It's easter morning
and last night the sky released oceans
hail lightning floods

almost biblical—
I didn't know how the four little eggs
would survive but I prayed
to whatever gods bring birds
for four safe little blue possibilities
this morning,
Easter,
a resurrection,
some sort of miracle
that our house Noah's arked them through the night,
and they were all alive and okay
and maybe I am mixing up my bible stories.

I ladder up to their weathered woven house,
fear that tragedy might await me
as I perch up on a stool
and tippy-toe stretch my toes
and wingspan my pointy fingers
hover-clutching iPhone camera
to survey storm damage to empty nest
and where are the parents,
where are bluebird mom and dad waiting in the trees?

Three little hatchlings
and one bright blue egg,
the hatchlings pink and newborn
hugging in a lifeless pile
wet
drowned
next to their unopened brother,
no parents in sight.
I wonder how long the mother will grieve.

Nature is cruel sometimes, Kai

my lover says from the window
and I weep into the morning,
resurrection denied,
rolling away the stone of day

to find three dead blue babies downy and gone,
still beautiful in their almosting

and this is not an image I wanted
to send out into this day,
but it's a reminder
that sometimes,
out of nowhere
everything can get washed away.

⌘ What Stitches Us Together

"There's a real beauty in that. The fabric we were going to use for people who died is now going to be used for people, hopefully, to live." — Gert McMullin (one of the two first volunteers that started the AIDS Memorial Quilt project in San Francisco in 1987)

Leftover pieces of the AIDS Memorial Quilt
are being used to make masks for COVID-19
and I knew this was a poem before I ever started writing it,

something about the full circle of a rainbow,

the story of these extra scraps of remembrance,
finding their way to faces now seeking protection,
these LGBTQuiltings coming back around to save us,

and this is not the first pandemic
these rainbow threads have weathered,
3 x 6 x 48,000 panels,
the size of an average grave,
and those are just the AIDS cases
tied to faces and names,
millions of beautiful humans erased,
no— this is not the first pandemic
these rainbow threads have weathered,
but there is something in the tragic beauty
of what they are stitching back together.

On the news, Dr. Fauci speaks at the podium
defends our courage against extraordinary stigma,
shines a light on our humanity and disparity,
reflecting on the Black and brown bodies
succumbing disproportionately in this current tragedy,
all while standing next to a vice president
who would rather pray the gay away
or shock it out of us with conversion therapy,
and where does a rainbow go when it dies?

Right now there are healthcare workers
wearing quilted masks on their faces,
these leftover blankets of memory
these precious swaths of color
are being given a new purpose in this unfolding,
the pieces of rainbows color everything golden,

maybe this gesture
can stitch our country back together,
maybe seeing each others'
humanity
and fragility
can stitch our country back together.

If any of my colors could help you,
I'd offer a part of my rainbow
to see you through.

⌘ Steadfast

The sun glares bright
this morning over the garden,

heavy and wet soil
still dark from last night's rain,

I expect the tertiary leaves
newly sprouted on our seedlings

to be battered and flattened
against the dawning,

but they stand tall as day,
thick-stalked and claiming their space in the sun,

their neon green faces pointed skyward,
determined to grow, steadfast with knowing

we will all get battered some days
our leaves and color torn to shreds

the weight of the world heavy
on our weary little heads

but in the morning (and after the mourning)
there will again

be
the sun.

⌘ Fledglings

she brought me outside the way she always does
on the cusp of some miracle

be very quiet
she whispered as we turned the corner of the back deck
to peek at the front door

the mother wren
who we have watched for weeks
quick with worms for her tiny criers
had corralled her babies into the hanging ivy plant
that drapes over the window by our front door

this was the big day to test their wings
pocket-sized parachuters anxious for a sky dive

the little chime of wrens huddled close in the pot
testing their brave as we watched from just feet away

it's not really flying
more like a slow
f
  a
    l
      l
        i
          n
            g
the way a feather drops from the sky
but this time a chunky baby bird
is attached to that very first try

one jumps from the lip of the ivy
like a weighted furry balloon
another

another
another fledged full

and mother wren sings
her praises
to every molecule of air

⌘ Smiling With My Eyes

There are over a million cases now,
I don't even have to name it anymore,
how it has spread into all of my poems like a contagion
and we don't know who among us is carrying this ungodly crown,
when we walk the once-safe spaces of our town,
when we socially distance our grocery trips,
all flowing down in one direction like little frightened ships,

but no man is born to be an island,
and I am aching to make contact,

six feet away,
six feet away,
please stand six feet away
or you'll be six feet under in an early grave,

what an interesting paradox,
but this time has so many of those—

doing NOTHING to save another
   like the president,

doing nothing to SAVE another
   like all of us shuttered in our homes,

sheltered in place,
our six degrees of separation hold much more meaning now.

And what about meaning—
hasn't *everything* changed?
hasn't our whole paradigm shifted?
everything that we know,
all of our definitions are twisted and turned
in this new dimension of unknown.

We casually tell complete strangers to *stay safe.*

We begin e-mails with *I hope you and your family are healthy.*

We watch as the unfathomable numbers grow and grow.
There is no where to put our dead.

Doesn't that old world we long for
seem like a distant memory that's lost its tangibility?

Look how now we cringe when we see commercials
of people in crowds all carefree
with their breaths and their hands and their laughter!

Look at our hearts race
when we see old group pictures,
(God, I miss group pictures)
squeezing into tiny frames,
no I can't see your head,
get in tighter,
get closer,
squeeze
say cheese! CHEESE!

But that was then
in the old world
pre-quarantine
47 days ago for me,
or is it 87?
is it time to eat again?
and what day is it?
week?
month?
it's May?

2020 vision is wearing fear-colored glasses and seeing the world through tears.

All the whiskey is gone,
and no this is not easy for anyone,
and we all wear our collective grief in different ways,
in different shades of collective grey,
and it is going to be a long time until all of this goes away.

So for today—
I go to the grocery store for supplies,
wear my mask like a good citizen,
hold my hand sanitizer
like a lump of salvation in my pocket,
move through the produce section
the way that a magnet repels another magnet,
regret touching a cantaloupe to see if it is ripe,
the hyper-cognition of touch
of space
of whatever you do
don't touch your face!

I find myself talking to myself as I move through the store,
like whispering into a seashell and hearing the ocean talk back,
my own mumbling in a sea of would-be bank robbers,
half-faced strangers, silent shoppers.

I am a smiler and a small-talker,
I am a hugger and a handshaker,
none of which matter in this world,
and all that is left uncovered
above my mask
are my eyes,
and if eyes are windows to the soul,
then let mine be all the way open.

This morning in the mirror,
I practiced smiling with my eyes,
put my hand over my mouth
and smiled with just the top half of my face
visible in the reflection,
and I admit it takes practice
to not look like you are just shocked
or your eyebrows itch
or you're curious
and maybe smiling with your eyes
means just stopping and looking deeper,
holding a stare where there once was a hand,

looking deep into another's window
when the smile is muted behind mask,

in this time of disconnection and pan(dem)ic,
it's one little thing I am going to consciously do,
look at people in the eyes
until they feel my smile coming through.

⌘ Unbouyant

When there are no more tears for the dying,
where does all of that salt go?

Does it melt back into the bodies of all who are left?

Do we swallow down an ocean
for her, and her, and him,
and brother, papa, auntie, love?

Do we become more buoyant in our numbness?

How do we memorialize the names of 85,000 strangers?
Even just to say all of their names
out loud in a stream would take days upon days.

Can you imagine how long their lives would be
strung end to end like that,
like those paper dolls that hold hands
unraveled, all their names,
one after another
like a sentence—
not a death sentence
but one that reads like a dream,
like a poem of everything beautiful they ever conceived,
or a string of all their 85,000 smiles
and how it would stretch and reach out for miles,
or let's line up every time they smelled something cooking
and it warmed them up inside,
or a poem of all of their dancing and romancing
and enchanting the fate of all their fallen stars
to give them a little longer on earth
than the 85,000 dead numbers they are.

They died alone.
That's the part that guts me.

Most of them died alone
while their families were locked down
not around, visitors are not allowed
to be there to hold their hands,
hand to hand to hand
unraveled,
separated isolated obfuscated,
no one should have to die like that,
fill up freezer trucks with their cut-short lives like that,
stack up black body bags to the sky like that.

Yet here in America the numbers still rise
while states reopen to capitalize
because the American Dream is there for the chasing
and there is no quarantine strong enough to stop this erasing
of lives
because half of us wear masks and stay home
and half of us (them) think it's all just a lie.

Round and round this plague will flow,
where it stops nobody knows,

but mark this day for all of the dead
and mark tomorrow
and tomorrow
and tomorrow after that.

When there are no more tears for the dying,
where does all of that salt go?

Does it melt back into the bodies of all who are left?

Do we swallow down an ocean
for her, and her, and him,
and brother, papa, auntie, love?

Do we become more buoyant in our numbness?

Because today I sit at a table of salt,
I turn back to their names and become a pillar of salt,
I open my hands and search
for paper dolls
fallen stars
      something
           someone
                to reach back.

⌘ Not Enough Words for Light

It is the first time
we have ever gone camping,
twelve years we have been roughing it
in our own personal heaven
on earth
home outside
with all of our wild,
but never like this,
in a tent
with the night building quiet
around a campfire.

There are logs burning
crackling like our tongues
against the darkening sky
and you tell me
we will be able to see
the Milky Way from here,
it is one of those lights-out campsites
that cultivates stargazing
and a galaxy hangs
from my heart
and spins
toward you.

A veil of lights
drops
or lifts
or suddenly manifests
from the ground up
and all around us,
as though pinprick holes
were cut in the grass and trees,
everywhere
there are tiny dances of floating light,

not just summer night firefly light
but every branch of every tree
lit up and sparkling,
like glimmer never knew
its definition
until now.

We walk across the meadow
to sit on the hood of the car,
a drive-in movie
of movement and flight,
we face the wall of trees
that hugs us from all sides
and we chase the shooting flames
of bioluminescent beings seeing each other,
calling out with the sex of their colors,
blinking their lust like a song
into the breaking-open night,
oh, to make light
out of our bodies
like this
just by breathing,
chemicals reacting like this,
like us,

and how the light show
becomes a blur
because above the tree-line
spread across the dome of night
are millions of flickering stars
all shimmer and shine
speaking the same language as the fireflies,
illumination rippling up and out
in cosmic waves,
a slow dance into the infinite
from grass to trees
to glinting sky

and there are not enough words for light

to embody this moment,
not enough synonyms for shine
to describe something this divine

and yes, we sat in wonder
and maybe we slow-danced
and maybe we kissed
and poets wait
their whole lives for
love scenes like this,

and even in this earnest retelling,
remembering sleep
underneath all those stars,
rolling over into your arms
and waking up covered in dew,
my smile is the Milky Way
you can see from here,
and it shines, darling—

it shines for you.

⌘ When the Stars Fall

the rain falls
hard heavy
on the white petals
of jasmine
that have entwined
their soft bodies to the steel
that holds our house
to the earth
swirling galaxy of stars
that affixes
us to the ground
and to the heavens combined

in the morning
a universe is scattered
under our bare feet

⌘ Makeshift Memorial

We crossed over the 100,000 mark
like it was just another Tuesday,
no fanfare no flourish of flowers left
on 100,000 graves, funeral-less limbo
walkers who disappear like a fog
into the history we are writing with our collective
inadequacy to be decent to each other.

A memorial is an object which serves as a focus
for the memory or the commemoration of something,
usually an influential, deceased person
or a historical, tragic event. (Wikipedia)

From behind a mask
I whisper 100,000 names
on the day we call Memorial,
because something should be done
to remember the living as they slip away,
the uptick in numbers that were never just numbers
but bodies full of breath
full of breath
     full of breath
        full of breath
knees and arms, ankles and bellies,
cheeks that dimpled at smiles,
gaps in teeth,
snores when she sleeps,
feet that once learned to tango,
earlobes once kissed in moonlight,
curls of hair silkened to white,
his aching back that worked so hard in the field,
her childbearing hips leaving children behind,
hands and hands and hands
that reach for mine in my mind,

not just numbers but human beings

reduced
      reduced
            reduced
until the only common denominator
is how quickly they are forgotten in this pandem(ic)onium.

I can't sit with that, no not today.
On Memorial Day we remember those who fought for our country and died,
but half the country forgot those fighting in ICU beds just to stay alive,
the collective death toll of our last four wars
and half of the country
doesn't want to quarantine anymore.

100,000 dead while America throws pool parties,
beaches and boardwalks swarm with shoulder to shoulder crowds
who dismiss the safety of the future for the party of now
because
this is America!
Land of the Free!
and don't tread on me!
and nobody is going to tell me to wear a mask!
and all of those soldiers
who died in all of those wars
I guess America can tell them it's too much to ask
to protect one another and help slow the spread
so happy Memorial Day— 100,000 dead.

A mass grave of indifference.

Red-capped rebels drinking their bleach cocktails.

And they are here, banging on the door
of my reverence to the lost,
waving their AR-15s on the capitol steps of this poem,
and I breathe them out
      and I breathe them out
            and I breathe them out.

I build a makeshift memorial
in my heart for the lives we have lost,

photos and teddy bears and scraps of poems,
I light 100,000 candles in the pit of my ribcage
so that when I speak, only the light of them releases
into the dark night of this country.

I dance with their 100,000 ghosts,
I lay their favorite flowers at all of their perfect feet,
in the language of heart I know their favorite flowers,
and I lay a bright she-loves-me petal on each of their lips
so they can breathe easy the ethers of beauty
while they rise into becoming anew.

We have to give them that grace,
even just a thought,
a well wish into the stars.

We have to give them that grace.

Tomorrow in America,
a new story named George will take our focus,
will move us into fury
or collapse us into numbness,
but today
I am a makeshift memorial,
a mouth full of epitaphs,
a funeral pyre
burning the sound of 100,000 names
into the history of a country
too quick to forget.

⌘ Black

The last poem I wrote
was to mark myself makeshift memorial
for 100,000 dead Americans.

That was three weeks ago
to the day,
and look at the street sweepers
brushing it all under the rug.

20,000 more into the nameless air
without a bat of presidential eyes,
the sound of cries dissipating
like a fog lifting
off the mo(u)rning.

In the span of three weeks,
look at how our world has changed.

George Floyd lived
and died
then bloomed
a new/old movement.

Millions took to the streets
and turned over new leaves within themselves,
started seeing hate and racism
with the rose-colored lenses of privilege finally taken off,
blinding themselves with the reality of
I CAN'T BREATHE and knee and neck and now,
the now that has always been,
when the color of your skin
is Black

Now—
Black is a movement,

Black is a battle cry,
Black is coming together,
Black is you and I
fighting for the justice every human deserves,
Black is all our voices marching, no longer unheard.

⌘ Plume

I am thinking about the way
the African dust is blowing in
from the sub-saharan continent
a plume that is consuming our skies
and how this hasn't happened in half a century

dust
of a desert
across an ocean
and we are breathing in
the particles of sand and life
and heat and strife
from a desert
calling to her stolen children—

if they can't come home to the Motherland,
         I   will   cross   the   sea   for   them   to   breathe

to breathe
to breathe
her in
with every breath
and yes it's making our sunsets
golden
and pink
and purple
the hues coming in
that wouldn't normally be in view
but maybe this isn't about sunsets
maybe this isn't about you
the haze like a warm gauze
over the open wound of this country
beautiful

or maybe this is here to show us

we are all still so connected
that nothing ever really disappears
that water evaporating
from the tears
on our face
just goes into space
to fall down again as rain
this cycle of letting go the pain
and pulling in and dropping down again
maybe this force
of nature
lifting up hundreds
of millions of tons of African soil
into the atmosphere and bringing it here
when we are at our most fear
is an unburial
an over-turn
a rebirth of earth
like the great gardener tilling the soil
singing her song for Emmett Till
and Tamir
and Trayvon
and Breonna
and Sandra
and Eric
and Freddie
and Ahmaud
and George
and Elijah
and and and
the infinity of hashtags
to rise into the
Motherland
Mother sand
Mother's hands

dust
that moves in the wind
to remind us of who we are when we end

and who we are when we begin
particles
particles of dust
painting the sunset a different color
red orange yellow hues
a fire in the sky

I breathe in Africa
I breathe in you

⌘ Izibongo for Black Women
(a praise poem after JP Howard, for my Sisters)

praise you Black Woman
because you never be praised enough
let me lift your collective name here
let me strip you of all your forced-on shame here
praise you for the stars that unfold when you smile
praise you for the way moons rise in your eyes
praise you for your tragic hope and sacrifice
life for you ain't been no crystal stair
but you still keep climbin' on
praise Langston's mama
praise her wisdom and truth

praise you Black Woman
because you never be praised enough
praise be your laugh
let me say that again because it's the song
that makes the planet spin
praise be your laugh
how it cackles and coos loud brassy beautiful
unafraid and unbroken
honey and fire

praise you Black Woman
because you never be praised enough
praise your natural hair and its curls
how whole galaxies swirl in the furls of you
praise your box braids and your twist outs
praise your locs and your bantu knots
praise how I got a Sister whose afro blocks out the sun
praise how I got another Sister whose afro is so tall
God uses it for a microphone
infuses her as gospel
Black Woman
praise your fingers braiding and trading beads

and weaving histories into wild glorious hair
the ceremony of pulling
praise your pulling
praise your pushing
pushing back on all that no longer makes room
for your crown
here Queen— here is your crown

praise the Motherland of your womb
how everything comes from you
and is stolen from you
and is returned to you again in glory
or entombed
I can't begin to know your story but
praise you Black Mama
forgive us for what we have done
and all that we still do
how we don't do right by your Black sons
how they are followed all their lives
by the shadows of guns
and how your Black daughters atlas the weight
of systemic cycles yet undone
and you still teach them to lift their faces to the sun
praise Breonna Taylor right here

praise you Black Woman
how you still raise continents of sons and daughters
despite their predisposition to being slaughtered
how the Atlantic ocean is still found in your transatlantic tears
the salt of you betrayed and splayed out
creating lands under your feet from all your centuries of grief
praise you as homeland
praise you as shore of a brighter world
praise the holy map of you
praise the North Star
that hangs from your earlobe like a pearl
praise you Black Mama
for how you hold the world
praise your swaddle and thick body

your warmth and your song
how you lullaby the night with a defiant hope
praise your hope
praise your dreams
praise the scripture of your face
praise the lines on your hands and crows-feet hymns
make an altar of my tongue
so that my words are poetic reparation
burn nag champa and sage in praise of your fire
praise be your fire
praise your persistence and your resistance
praise how you Harriet your children to a new freedom
praise how you Rosa until someone else offers you a seat at the table
praise how you Audre deliberate and afraid of nothing
praise how you Maya rising and phenomenal
praise how I got a Sister who named her daughter Revolution
Black Woman praise you
how your heroes and saints speak to you from the edge of the world
how your ancestors tell you the mountaintop is near
how every step toward freedom
is emblazoned into your DNA
encoded in your retaliations of Black Joy
praise your Black Joy
praise your Black Joy

praise you Black Woman
because you never be praised enough
praise your hips
praise your thighs
praise your arms and your legs
praise your back and your heavy head
praise your neck and them tight-ass shoulders
praise your temples
and how your whole beautiful Black Woman body
is a Temple
praise you Black Temple
praise your knees and your elbows
your fingers and your toes
praise your perfect beautiful Black nose

and your perfect lips
praise your voice that sings and hums and *hallelujahs*
praise your voice that shouts for justice
that leads us all to shout beside you ***BLACK LIVES MATTER***

Sister praise you
praise your heart for all that you bear
praise your ears for all that you hear
praise your eyes for all that you see
how your eyes and ears sometimes
bring you your biggest fears
and yet somehow somehow you soldier on
praise you Black Woman
I don't know how you be so strong
I don't know how you be so strong

this praise poem could just go on and on and on and on
because Sister—you never be praised enough

⌘ Tell Me More

(for Amanda)

Tell me more
about being a goddess

the young girl says

and the earth mothers
come from the four winds
to lay down the veils of their firmament

out of mountains
a current of feminine light speaks

earth mother has hipbones
in the Himalayas
see them now snow-skirted
and sky cleared
of your machine breaths
      while you humans stay still
      locked down
her curves speak of hope

earth mother has lips
in sunrises that dawn
every day as unwritten
full of potential and possibility
red and golden

earth mother has breasts
that spill milky ways
galaxies born
from the breadth of her
chest swept with stars
a nursery of nebulas nearing bloom

earth mother has arms
as wide as all the oceans
vast and limitless
in the children she carries
their names each a cell dividing into tomorrow

earth mother has feet
that have born canyons grand
into the supple land
walked in each of our human stories
see how she traverses our experience

earth mother has starry eyes
that have witnessed
all we have done to her
still— she prisms
and bends astral light around creation
hoping that beauty can restore our goodness

earth mother has hands
that cup and hold
and shape and build
redwood fingers glacial nailbeds
tectonic prayers only for us

earth mother has a heart
that is every volcano pulsing
every eruption forming new land
over what it has burned
again and again spewing lava and love
to recreate islands that Pangea us together again

How can I be a goddess one day?

the young girl asks

and an aurora bends down
from the northern lights

to her ear saying *child*—

every goddess is an earth mother
and every mother is the earth
and every child has earth
hidden in its name
in the sounds between vowels
that speak in the language of water

⌘ Palette

last night
before sleep
she drew pictures on my back
with her fingers
a test of my spacial recognition
my ability to form
a horse
a sun
a sailboat
from the movement of her fingertip traces
against my skin
to see it
take shape in my mind's eye
invisible palette

the curvature of my back
competing with her delicate design
of flower
fish
smile
and I cannot guess
cannot translate the trace to shape
each time she erases
whole palm swipes in the dark
tries again
rabbit
snail
and I am the worst at this game
because
just being touched
by the fingertip of this artist
just having my skin rise to meet her

all I can picture in these traces is

Heaven

Heaven

Heaven

⌘ Gravitation

perhaps my heart is your moon
circling the light and grace
by which you
anchor
and
pull me
close
closer
closer still
the orbit of this love
a magnet spin for two

perhaps my face finds a place to belong
in the way you move as a world of your own
planet of compassion
spinning rock of wonder
movement of light
you spread so much beauty into me
I can only moon-mirror bounce the light
back into you with these poem-song-howls of thanks

gravitational is all I can use to explain
the force of my pull to your heart
your heavenly bodies
the open sky of your eyes
holding every sunrise my name has ever known

the phases of my love
are always full
full
and fuller
never more complete
than this cycle
this dance
around the planet of you

pull
pull me
pull me in
never let me go

⌘ Filling Spice Jars As Your Wife

It seems like all my poems
after this will be different,
they will hold a different weight
like how the weight of my heart
has shifted into indistinguishable float,
into lifting cloud,
into weightless flight tonight
as the rain gently falls
on the summer-heated tin roof,
the din of casual raindrops
and warm low lights glowing
and wind blowing through the house,
we have all our doors and windows open.

We have all our doors and windows open
and I am pouring spices into glass jars,
coriander cinnamon cumin ground sage
and it's hard to describe this
moment in the confines of a page,
tiny hills of vibrant color
and intoxicating fragrance
and you hear the cadence
of my heart
from the kitchen
where you build perfect fitting slip-in shelves
for our spices over the stove,
match the colors,
match my colors to yours,
I have all my doors and windows open to you.

I have all my doors and windows open to you
and you have come all the way inside,
sat down at the table of my deepest desires
and lit a fire to warm us both,
the wind blowing through the house,

the rain gently giving way
to turmeric sunrise
and you, darling,

you are my wife.

You are my wife
and it's like I have been waiting
my whole life
to say those words,
and I feel held in a way
I have never felt before,
to look down at my fingers
dusted with ginger and thyme
and see the gold of my wedding band
glint and shine in the warm low light glow,
I am yours
and you are mine,
promised on Zoom in our garden
of giant zinnia and hummingbird vines,
sung out in the morning song of bluebirds,
this union that ripples love out to the world
and infinities back into us again
love —
in the fine powder of these spices,
ground up essence of oregano and basil,
I see our love in every atom suddenly
and every cell in me finally exhales,
and perhaps that is the wind.

Perhaps that is the wind
blowing through the house,
this release of eternal searching
and finding you there,
calling me your forever,
naming me your always,
to have and to hold,
till death do we part and start all over again
looking only for each others' hearts,

taking my life in your hands eternal,
marrying me to the heavens,
latching me to the star-trail of your white dress,
in this orbital dance,
this lift and spin,
this knowing from within
that all my poems after this will be different

because you are my wife.

⌘ Saying My Wife At Every Possible Occasion, After We Get Married

wife
my wife
this is my wife
this is my wife Joann
my wife Joann and I wake up together
my wife and I water the garden in the morning
my wife and I pick a huge harvest of our veggies grown from seeds
it starts to rain but my wife and I like the rain
my wife and I keep picking veggies drizzled in joy
beans cucumber squash blossoms a little army of short fat-legged carrots
colors explode in my wife's perfect hands
my wife and I go inside and dry each other off
I kiss my wife in the foyer
my wife and I slow dance in the kitchen
my wife fries up bright yellow squash blossoms in a little olive oil and salt
my wife makes suns rise in my mouth

I wrote my name and "wife" on the dry erase board
the emergency contact in ICU before all this pandemic
when I almost lost her
and when she woke up from almost death
there it was "wife" the first thing she saw
and after 13 years now it is true

the first full day of being married
I think I call her *my wife* 314 times or infinitely
and my wife thinks it's cute
that I say *my wife* at every possible occasion now until forever

and in every poem from the past
where I have called her
darling
my love
sun moon and all the stars

I want to go back and edit those words to *my wife*

because my wife
is now
and always has felt like
and always will be
my wife

⌘ Ring Sing

There is a new song
that comes from my fingers,
a new vibration
as the sound
of my promise clinks
against the everyday things
I hold and touch,

the sound my wedding ring makes
against a glass,
a tiny bell of hope,

the song it makes as I
swipe the sudsy stainless steel sink,
push wet carrot tops
and bean ends
into the garbage disposal
with this soft scrape of gentle forever,

I keep hearing
what I think are bells,
but it is just my
ring
singing
into everything.

⌘ Aperture *(chasing NEOWISE)*

I wrote this poem
before I wrote this poem,
already saw it taking shape in the sky,
scooped the words
out of the mouth of the big dipper,
light written in stars
on a mountaintop next to you,

we chased the comet
for three days looking for cloudless clearings
and wandering northwest toward a horizon
we could find ourselves in,
on the star trail of a comet that rises
to meet us every 6,800 years,
and my love, tonight we are here
just up the mountain road by our house,
the theater of galaxies
at the top of our darkened street,

the clouds dissipate into clarity and
the heavens open up
to a grandeur
that can only come
once
in a lifetime,
the paw of a great bear coming down
to touch our faces,
to brush our wild eyes with gold,

we lay in the middle of the street,
tilted up like a pasha pillow
in plain view of the firmament,
we drink in the twilight
knowing the tail of light trailing behind a burning star
and the falling crescent kissing the tops of pines

will dance for hours
and we are here, and you are mine

all I think of in this moment is aperture,
how my camera
can slowly inhale the stars
in a long exposure
and my long exposure
to you
has only taught me
the concept of opening fully
to let all the light in,

when the world is flooded with
so much darkness
what else can we chase
but the stars,
but the blooming cosmos
flower in the garden,
the bumblebee,
the lark song in the trees,

tonight
there is a double meteor shower
raining fire in the sky
you are building a tent outside
as I finish writing this poem

and I will chase
all the light with you

I will chase all the light with you.

Aperture open wide.

⌘ Microcosm Macrochaos

The other night in the bedroom before sleep
I rescued a drowning firefly from the water bowl,

listened to my little dog thirsty purring in the dark
and got up to bring the bowl to the bed for her to drink,

and there it was— this slow swimming swirling light
this blinking of almost giving up

and I scooped it out with my fingers,
its drenched wings draping over my fingerprints with thanks.

In most species of firefly, only the females will blink
and her sweet cold light was dimming so I walked her to the screen door

and let her see the almost full moon, cold light reflection,
as I held her on my fingertips warming her with my body.

I blew on her and unstuck her little wings and she moved
and glowed between the valleys of my fingers, the lines of my palm,

her light growing brighter and brighter as the minutes passed.
I brought her in to show my family in bed— *look she's ok! Layla saved her!*

My wife looked at the flickering light in my hand
and Layla sniffed the strengthening little being softly.

I walked outside and put the rescued firefly on a leaf
thanked her for her beauty and wished her a nice life.

This is the tenderness in which we live. We listen to the creatures.
Every tiny speck of life is given the respect and love and space it needs.

We let a spider live outside in the corner of our front door for two weeks.
Each day at dusk he would weave his elaborate web over the entrance to our house,

81

his artwork blocking the doorway, face full of silk
if you were to run through without noticing, every morning all cleaned up,

and we let him stay, named him Dorian Intheway
because he was in the way and a picture of the life we live every day,

giving him a safe space despite our fears, and it only taught us
there was never anything to be afraid of in the first place.

He started weaving his web with just the exact space underneath it
for us to walk under without catching silk, mutual, symbiosis, give and take,

live and let live, let live, let live— Dorian left for a new house a few days ago,
but what a lesson he wove into the space of our coming home.

This it the tenderness in which we live. We listen to the creatures.
Every tiny speck of life is given the respect and love and space it needs.

In America, 1,000 people are dying a day
while COVID tightens its fingers around the throat of our country

They are dying, that's true— It is what it is
shouts the emperor with no clothes holding his charts proclaiming we are great

OPEN THE SCHOOLS!! he tweets in all caps
and in Georgia a photo of a packed hallway of high school kids goes viral—

viral like a school of fish swimming to slaughter,
viral like 50 million kids about to swirl around in a petri dish disaster,

viral like let's send in the teachers to die for the economy,
their lives are expendable and children don't get the virus anyway, right?

In Beirut an explosion reduces the entire city to rubble
thousands are injured, hundreds are dead, they just haven't been found yet,

and a mushroom cloud of grief rises from my heart
for the dead falling in the mass grave this earth is so quickly becoming,

so many souls caught in the ethers, blasted out of the sky,
dying alone strapped to a ventilator, or exploded into fragments,

and there is such a devastating chasm between my microcosm and the macrochaos
I can only find hope and infinity here in the infinitesimal—

holding a blinking firefly in my hand, breathing it back to life,
calling it a poem.

⌘ *This America,* How Much More Can We Take?

it's a constant painful inundation
to be alive in this America
this America
as if I have detached myself from   my country
as if I am removed
from its borders
outsider trapped inside
warrior of light with no where to hide—
how much more can we take?

this America—
its spacious skies
choked with the ash of a million acres burning
climate change deniers keep the fires raging higher
everything tinder
everything silver cinders and smoke
black out the sun with the arms of falling redwoods
ancients collapsing
with the weight of humanity's collective disregard—
how much more can we take?

this America—
its amber waves and waves of pain
every day a new horror
every day a new shame
another slashing of our human dignity
by the hands of the heartless minority in (stolen) power
a regime that viciously stamps out American dreams
and builds walls of broken glass and silenced screams
brandishes weapons of fear and hate and teens with AR-15s
turns our stars into swastikas in the bright of day
this is America 2020 and I cannot look away
he turns the peoples' house white white white white
holds an authoritarian ego convention on the sacred steps with flood lights
blinding out the darkness he created as savior for the radical right—
how much more can we take?

this America—
from sea to (once) shining sea
we are a sick country quarantined
suffocating in a public health emergency
our passports no good for travel internationally
because we have no handle on this ravaging disease
300,000 will die before the end of the year
the world laughs at our dictator in chief
as he says what a very good job he did
the very best job ever he did
better than any other country ever he did
better than humanly possible and every other fucking superlative
the most robust testing (lie)
it will just disappear (lie)
china virus china virus china virus (racism)
I provided the most ventilators and PPE (lie)
cases are going up because testing is going up (gaslighting)
maybe try drinking some bleach (seriously?)
hydroxychloroquine (oh please)
I will have the best vaccine (lie)
children are virtually immune (lie)
and we send in the teachers to die for the economy—
how much more can we take?

this America—
its purple mountain majesty turned bloody bruises
turned tear gas and rubber bullet blush
turned crush under the foot of brutality's boot
knee on his pleading throat
George
shot seven times in the back in front of his children
Jacob
these men
these Black men
these Black fathers
whose martyrdom is unfounded
unfound fathers lost to their existences
holes

in their former lives
to teach us a lesson
that just keeps repeating and repeating
that you cannot be Black in *this America* and survive
you cannot be sleeping like Breonna Taylor and stay alive
hashtags stitched up to the stars like barbed wire
and we have fenced ourselves in
with all our collective history and hate
to look at each other in the face
until each side screams
for a civil war
and *this America*—
I just can't take anymore

I just can't take it anymore

anyone with a heart in their chest
a pulse in their striving soul
a light inside that guides them
can see us
            all of US
spiraling out of control

how much more can we take?
how do we save our principles?
how do we build upon real foundations
while there are monsters tearing at the roots?
how do we save our democracy our liberties our virtues?
how do we taste hope on our lips again?

Vanquish the oligarch and his mob of evil men
Open your heart even wider though it may be broken
Tell truth to power though your voice might be shaking
Embolden justice progress inclusiveness brotherhood empathy and light

This is still Our America

This is still Our America

And we are still in this fight

⌘ The Language of Hitting Bottom

I wept at the south rim of the Grand Canyon,
rising over the ridge line to my very first sight of it

the tears poured from my eyes like something was unbroken,
like there was still a miracle that could awe me into silence,

I stood on the edge of the world, warm-blooded and alone,
as if I was a priest of the infinite and its prayer at the same time,

every atom in me genuflected at the expanse of all this stripping away,
and this chasm of time swallowed me whole with its vastness and depth,

I tossed an acorn into the wishing well of it all,
waiting to hear the sound of hitting a bottom it would never reach,

the echo of oak not yet manifest into shade
but I listen for what hits the rock bottom of what I know—

that the infinite cannot be tested, that nature has its own language,
and most of us still speak in the dialect of want and need,

while canyons whisper in the rush of untranslated water and trees,
and this poem was meant to be about wonder, and I went back

to the Grand Canyon in my mind, stood there overcome,
but depths are inextricably linked to other depths, bottomless

reflections to the language of now, the whirling abyss of waking
in the depths of what is unfolding cannot shake from me, escape

from my poetry, I find myself on the precipice of some moral tightrope,
watching a COVID rose garden massacre ripple out sickness

to the morally sickest people, the leader who led this country
into the darkest darkness, breathing celebratory virus all over

nominated justice, against the dying wish of a supreme dissenter,
and they all reveled in their hypocrisy, exchanging toxic pleasantries

in the unmasked light of day, super-spreading their self-congratulatory
victories un-distanced from diseased mouths, and the language of all of this

does not escape me, the quantum entanglement of his criminal negligence
and hypocrisy, spinning with the particles of death droplets

in the immoral depth that never seems to hit bottom,
there is no bottom to the emptiness of his empathy,

the nut never hits bottom, the only echo back is the sound of his superlatives,
only the boasts and brags that he is the best, better than any leader before,

the roses weep with disdain for all that unfolds in the garden,
where men and women of compassion and good once stood, and now

the president has COVID, his first lady, press secretary, top advisors, all the generals
of every branch of the military, infected tree disjointed and quarantined,

all the king's horses and all of the king's men, together in the garden
super-spreading their political end, and I walk the tightrope beside karma

and nature's law, the medical evacuation from the white house lawn
to the best hospital in the world, and why does he get the best treatment

in the world, when he mocked the masked faces for months and spit on science,
a white coat cadre of enablers give him experimental drugs and pump his ego

with steroids so he can superhero himself back to the White House
in a grandiose display of recklessness and flagrant tyrannical pageantry,

and he tweets *Don't be afraid of COVID. Don't let it dominate your life.*
while 210,000 dead Americans roll over in their lonely still-warm graves,

and I listen for the justice that I know will come, I watch for the bend
of that moral arc of the universe coming back around, while the reality TV star's

helicopter touches back down on White House ground, the roses quiver and
I listen for the sound of the mad king hitting bottom, ascending the staircase

breathless, he rips off his mask in dramatic victory in the new infamous
balcony scene of our history, claims his *maybe I'm immune*-ity,

he'll be back to campaigning and debating and defacing our humanity,
and I am standing at the south rim of the loss of democracy,

tears in my eyes as the supreme court injustices toy with my life,
taking away my right to call the woman I love my wife,

I am walking the tightrope beside karma and nature's laws
listening, watching, waiting for the sound darkness of hitting bottom,

so the wishing well of justice can rise, wave, flood, tsunami blue
back into the divided canyon this country has become.

⌘ I Will Hold Onto Joy

We did it—
five days of waiting, watching, counting
to a definitive blue
and I shouted
to my bubble bathing wife
in the next room
we did it!
she splashed and screamed
and it's like I started to wake up
from a four-year bad dream
because suddenly
the truth was all there
in blue and more glorious blue
slowly sweeping across the states
that we did it,
that democracy won,
that all our voices mattered
united and strong,
a new American song
and we all knew the words to it all along.

I went out on the back deck
that faces our pond and the bottom of our valley,
surrounded on all sides
with rising stone and small mountain slopes,
surrounded on all sides
with those who wave red flags on the backs of pick-up trucks,
and I yelled at the top of my bright blue lungs

PRESIDENT JOE BIDEN!
VICE PRESIDENT KAMALA HARRIS!

I yelled it twice for good measure
like a little town cryer,
and it echoed like freedom beating a drum

into a captive night,
the stone bowl of our valley
becoming mountaintop touching sky,
inverted world tipping back on its axis of light,
I rang the temple bell outside eight times
and it reverberated an infinity of hope
into the limestone bluffs, suddenly sublimestone,
yes— tell every rock and grain of sand,
we are taking back our beloved country and reshaping it with open hands.

My wife and I danced in a zoom with our friends
while thousands danced in the streets,
laughter and song erupting
from a chorus of unbroken hope,
we kissed,
we drank champagne,
we tasted the colors of joy.

The world watched us topple a dictator,
we stood against a flailing tyrant
and democracy won,
our beacon unburdened
by his brainwashed militia,
our song unflinching against his 25,000 lies,
and though he will never concede
we know that we stood up with the power of the people
and the world watched us RISE.

It's like all the colors
were suddenly brighter,
the leaves on the trees shimmered
their golden fall hues
like they knew
that we did it,
that in the coming days
they would be safer to stand,
safer on their national protected lands,
that the air wouldn't be theirs to clean alone,
they danced on their branches,

waved through the windows
against the bluest sky
I had ever seen.

I've been bursting into tears for days now,
like a drastic untangling of knots in my stomach,
like I can un-wring my hands and know when I reach out,
my America will be there to hold me,
like I have been in abuse survival mode for four years
watching every day the dismantling of goodness,
preparing for daily gut punch headline,
burning from all the gas being lit inside me,
the anxiety the fear the fight the righteous rage,
the hundreds of children locked in a cage,
the planet screaming *please listen, I'm dying,*
Black Lives just trying to breathe against a backdrop of sirens,
and this country has been just too much to take,
but let it be written in our history books
that on Election Days 2020
we collectively erased an orange mistake.

I could write how the joy
ebbs into fear and anxiety still,
the destruction behind the scenes,
demagogue and his mob refusing to concede,
and how there will be seeds of chaos sown
into January fields,
but I won't go there in this poem,
I will hold onto joy,
I will hold onto joy,
I will hold onto joy.

I will remember seeing Kamala become
the brightest star
in a constellation of hope
for little Black girls,
for little South Asian girls,
for all little girls all over the world,
I will remember Joe and his vulnerable stutter

knocking down the Goliath Bully-in-chief
with a stone of unconquerable truth.
I will see that poetry is returning to the White House,
that our leaders will listen to science,
will cultivate a rose garden of progress,
will lead in a way that we will rise up behind and follow,
we will hold them to our will,
and they will listen
and fight not against us, but beside us
toward that fabled moral arc of the universe.

I can unclench my jaw,
I can breathe out the tightness in my chest,
I can roll back the tension in my neck,
I can drop the burdens I've carried so long on my shoulders,
I can cry oceans for all that we have lost
take the salt in my hands
throw it over my left shoulder
into the eyes of evil
and say *you will NOT enter this house again!*
as I walk with my head held high toward the sun,
I will sage this page of our story,
and I will hold onto joy,
I will hold onto joy.

I will close my eyes and see us all dancing in the streets,
when I get scared I will remember the dancing,
I will remember the dancing,
I will hear the echo in my valley,
I will hold onto joy.

I am not naive,
I know winter is coming,
and it may be dark and unwilling to move,
but come January 20th, at the strike of noon,

a lotus will bloom at our feet.

⌘ Mining for Stardust

there are stars in our eyes
like all of the constellations are convening
in the clearing our winter trees window
to the universe

I want to see the rings tonight
the rings of Saturn rounding all my sharp corners
but I can't see them with my naked eyes
so human and blurred
blue stars
appear over the horizon
before they fall
behind the evergreen tree line
and the indigo engulfs the moment

this grand conjunction
Jupiter and all of her moons
Saturn and all of her rings
yes tonight
on this solstice
the planets are *all* women
the stars too
pleiades hangs
like a plump fruit of light
from the branches stripped of leaves
and the half-moon beams down
her face half-shadowed by her own luminance

tonight is for the good witches
the covens of light pulsing
goddesses all over the country
all over the world
have fires to burn tonight
somewhere outside somewhere inside
whether they are only fires in their hearts

fires in their minds
what else does a goddess do during a solstice but make a fire?
so we bring our trees to this circle
and set them ablaze
dance and thump into the earth
howl at the empty fullness sparkling with stars

maybe the goddesses on Jupiter and Saturn
are looking here in this grand conjunction
looking at us in wild wonder
looking for signs of light
flickers of hope
streaks of greatness
a return
a calling to home

maybe we are all mining for stardust
sifting flakes of space for gold
amidst the dark matter
surrounding us on all sides

I shine
the brightest flashlight I have
(my heart)
into the night sky
shout *I am the Milky Way!*
to anyone that will hear me
I am cosmos
cosmic beauty
something of the firelight shooting into the sky
smoke rising from my mouth
fire glinting in my teeth
I look for a sign and I am the sign

the planets are lining up
so close on this solstice night
they look like one Bethlehemic miracle of a star
and I curl up so close to you
in the warm tent you have made for us fireside

fluffed with piles of soft blankets and pillows
our dogs snoring under starlight
the night is rife with poems
our nights always ripening into beauty
and maybe we are a conjunction's reflection
grand in our blue closeness
merging to naked eyes
on the horizon

as one

⌘ Brighter When Wet

My wife bought us bath salts from Germany,
deep colored rocks glowing in their jars,
one eucalyptus-arnica-rosemary-sun-gold,
the other valerian-hops in rich teal ocean midpoint depth,
the shade between sea floor and surface.

I reach for the teal, almost always,
sing in the shades as the waterfall of water
swirls in the hues of deep blues,
makes the smallest waves white capping in the bathtub,
steam rises and pulls me by the chin
to sink my body into this oceanic deep.

I remove the day, strip myself
of the expectations and the pain,
the way my soul strives and my flesh endures,
and I stand naked waiting to become this color.

I displace the waves with all my bodies,
from physical to divine I dive
into the teal song to feel in this new luminance,
to speak in shades of aqua and azure,
lapis lazuli and indigo,
and deeper *in* I go,
into the undertones of light bouncing
to the backs of my eyes,
oh, make me vivid, paint me blue,
skin soak this teal tinge into my cells, I beg you.

I am a soft whale singing the deeper and deeper I swim in these tones,
splashing like a slick fish wild with iridescence,
I soak hoping to be stained,
vying to be dyed in this end of the spectrum,
permeate me, imbue me with this hue
for I am Venusian, take me home,

my skin is normally a nebula,
the unspoken blue of the most outer space,
and I am an earthbound star, brighter when wet—
I pick up the light and remember.

⌘ Water for Martians *(scientists discover water on Mars)*

"There is no light in earth or heaven
But the cold light of stars;
And the first watch of night is given
To the red planet Mars." — *Henry Wadsworth Longfellow*

Tonight, my water broke
on your blood moon,
the sun's shadow
lifted up my dress, for eons
I have held my tongue,
but tonight I am liquid
red.

I held an ocean once,
carried its moving waves
in my chest,
dried up,
rising up and out into space,
my mouth a sea floor,
my breasts these
volcanic iron-rich mounds
that nobody warm touches,
metal roving fingers prod for my secrets,
yes, I hold water.

At night,
there are star-filled puddles
of the clearest tears
that form on my rocky surface,
but there are no earth words
for this type of rain,
for this type of evaporation and drain,
my tides are invisible,
pulling inward what wants to flow,

I hold water,

there are tattooed tributaries
running the expanse of my skin,
but you cannot see the life
I have created with my spin,
my ovulating orbits,
my twin moons pulling me in directions
that make me almost earthly in my revolution,
my time, just as fleeting,
I hold water,
but it disappears
with each turn of my cheek
toward the sun,
my atmospheric veil too thin
to keep these prayers as moving rivers,
as a promise of microscopic sovereignty,
I hold water,

it moves through me
but your satellites cannot see
through my breaking,
something is birthing here
not for earthly eyes to see,
I am drawing in
and pushing out planetary   breath,
undulating on the inside
what the puddles cannot hide,
I hold water,

I hold life,
and I am not the namesake of War.
I am Woman,
metal rust blood water red life,
I am slowly
pulling in the infinitely
spinning elements of stars,
breathing in nebulas and
freezing eternal possibilities at my poles,

I hold water,

I hold creation yet to be,
I hold rising tides underneath
that will flood into oceans, you'll see,
my veil will be lifted,
my name,

Future.

⌘ I Find My 2020 Glasses from New Years

I find my 2020 glasses from New Years—
silver and plastic, they tumble out of the art closet

to the floor, their tangible irony hangs at my ankles.
I pick them up, move them in my hands (shiny, unthreatening),

slip them onto my face this icy late December full moon night,
look back through the lens-less lenses with cold curious senses,

to see what I can see, to look back on this year that's changed us all,
and the last time I wore these glasses, I wished for clarity,

but I didn't mean it like this, I didn't mean 2020 perfect vision
making everything that mattered suddenly come into blinding focus,

I blink and 2020 floods the backs of my eyes, reckless and cruel,
the reflective mirror sheen infinities me into flashback loops,

a gold star diagonals my left eye and the zeroes open eye holes,
the first 2 juts my right cheekbone and the other 2 bridges my nose,

a year spelled out silver on my face, spelled out on all our faces in the letters
of the lost, the sounds of their names, the holes we heavy—

and maybe there is symbolism in the positioning of these signs,
cheap drugstore party favor turned crystal ball visionary rhymes,

and I have tried to come to this poem from all possible sides,
wanted to mark this year with something meaningful that I write,

but the words just don't come, no matter the hum of my brain turning
over the days in my hands, I'm numb, I breathe, I breathe again—

I pain over the lines, and sometimes a poem can't paper cup oceans,
or see the clarity in 2020 glasses at the end of this darkest year,

trying to pen some clever flip of a script none of us knew the words to,
year that cut us off at the knees, made us grieve, and question deeply our beliefs,

these frames that name all the pain and growth we've blamed on a year
that dropped all the balls on us, dumpster-fire-hell-scape we called living,

the socially-distant-my-god-I miss-you-please-don't-die we called surviving
and all I can think of is 2020's grand design began with wildfires,

over a billion animals in Australia burnt to bushland black,
devastation starting in the animal kingdom, their spirits phoenixing,

and I taught a poetry class to children here, while children there cried
under red apocalypse skies and I wrote a poem— "Koala in Past Tense"

should've dedicated it us, precursor to a year of staring down tenses,
becoming present, becoming past, hoping desperately for a future,

and the clues were forming in the fiery atmosphere, every paradigm
we knew was about to go up in flames, singe and wither, fall away,

then Kobe crashed into a mountainside, died on a January day, he was 41.
I turn 41 in two days and I see the shock wave of one man's death,

how one death seems to carry more weight than 339,000 in the tonnage
of grief, but how do I quantify something like that in a poem?

This is January, was January in the year of our lord *Oh Lord what now,*
and a billion animals hovering in the ethers saying *wait humans,*

your kingdom comes, and the plastic glasses on my face heavy
with each memory, slide into the cold of February when the first death

from COVID finds our shores, impeached president resident demagogue retains
his rei(g)ns on darkness and we go on in our untouchable americanness

thinking this virus is only in the otherlands, the autopilot of our lives about
to grind into a halted March. We watch Italians lock down, sing operas

from aching balconies, waters of Venice clear from lack of humans,
dolphins swim, and by Friday March 13th, I am hiding in a bathroom

in an elementary school between classes, waiting in fear of children's hands,
waiting for the school to shut down, then everything shuts down, locks

down and we mouth the words **global pandemic** for the first time.
Breonna Taylor was also shot that day, look how the storylines coincide.

We lose half our faces behind masks, scrub-scald our hands raw, wipe
down groceries, collectively hold breaths, as daily the deaths take us, take us.

April we shelter in place, howl nightly for essential workers, clap for heroes,
bang pots from balconies, and New York City piles with bodybags.

There is not enough space to bury all the dead, this pervading image
runs through my head, still peering through these 2020 eyes in dread.

May, mayday mayday we're crashing crashing, we can't breathe,
I CAN'T BREATHE George Floyd screams, neck under knee of brutality,

May, in masks we take to the streets, two pandemics— COVID-19 and Black men
historically being murdered by police, BLACK LIVES MATTER we shout

and hold protest signs, I see millions marching in this poetic rewind,
and in May we crossed over an unfathomable number— 100,000 dead

as science naysayers and red hats pool party for Memorial Day instead,
the peoples' divide widens, the 2020 glasses crack down the bridge,

June we topple confederates, battle literal nazis as tensions rise,
thousands more die, July and August is a summer of our own wildfires,

If only we swept the forest of dead leaves trump said, and *it is what it is*
when talking about the Americans dead, and there is a hope that rises

in the back of our masked throats, in a few months we'll all rise to **VOTE**
in the most influential election of all our lives, but from August to November,

we still have to survive, John Lewis and RBG cross over to fight
from the other side, trump tells the proud boys to *stand back and stand by.*

This reel to reel remembrance through 2020 party favor glasses
can't lose focus now, must see it all, can't lose the vision that

the division between those of us who believe in science and those
who balked at COVID compliance, drove us only further into graves,

another hundred thousand lives could've been saved, they said
goodbye to their families on iPads, choked on ventilators in ICU,

this was summer's other narrative, the untouchable deaths and what
loneliness can do, how we all became pixelated half-dressed bodies on zoom,

reaching out reaching out as we humans do. Let's skip to hope now,
the election won, vaccines, the words *light* and *tunnel,* the dark winter

blooming into possible spring, and I can see clearly now, I can see everything,
my 2020 perfect vision blurred with tears of everything lost,

but look at what we have also gained. Paradigm shifts rippling through
all of humanity take disaster and sometimes calamity, take breaking

and reshaping, dust returning to dust, fires burning everything
all at once, and maybe you found out what really matters this year.

Maybe all of us who survived and are still surviving, will have
the eyes to see, will have the hearts to heal, will have common

struggle and stories, just like in putting on these 2020 New Year's
glasses and remembering this painful glorious year, I see

that everything that mattered was already in front of me,
I married the woman I love, I wrote poetry, I fought like hell

for American democracy, I put my hands into the soil and
we ate vegetables planted from seed, I learned to identify

birdsongs singing from the trees, I stretched and I stretched
into a higher version of me— this was the gift of 2020.

You see, clarity comes in many forms. All of us, all at once
had the chance to see things more clearly, to hold closer

to our hearts what we really hold dearly, to learn and work
beside our growing children, to shape our own little worlds rebuilding.

I will keep this vision always, place the 2020 glasses on
my office bookshelf to remember the perceptions gained,

the higher insight suddenly ordained, the clarity of crystals
glimmering like stars in my eyes, guiding us all perhaps

to a better home, a better world,
on the other side of this year we survived.

⌘ Hummingbird Scout

It seems they are early this year,
the blizzard of February
maybe tipped the axis of things,
buds and blooms are askew,
their timing thrown off,
the expected parade of daffodils
tulips clover dogwood then the steady barraging
of all things pollen neon green, but this year it seems
all topsy-turvy in their outbursting from bare,
the trees singing over each other in their solos,
and now this— earliest little hummingbird
on the second day of April.

My love and I were out on the back deck
building some new dream with wood,
and like a blur in a second
a quick flash of sound
came inches from my face,
and I recognized the whirring,
didn't even see his little red ruby throat
but knew the song of his immeasurably fast wings,
and this is one of the things
that fills my gratitude space today
that begs to be laid into verse,
that we can recognize the blurred whirr
of the season's first hummingbird scout
telling us his friends are migrating back to us
and will be here soon.

The same little scout comes every year,
the reconnaissance blur of a bird
who makes sure we are ready for everyone,
a chubby stout Napoleon of a creature
who flies in to check the supply chain
in the anticipatory charm landing,

oh, by the way, the collective noun
for a group of hummingbirds is a charm,
and the charming thing is
I know that my wife
will drop what we are doing immediately
to dig out the feeders wintering in the kitchen cabinet,
she'll scoop out the sugar and
mix her special nectar right away for him,
not the red chemical stuff in the stores,
no never, but a perfectly blended ambrosia
of pulverized sugar and water swirled
and hung from a flower shaped welcome back feeder.

Charming.

We wait by the window,
see the scout perched tiny in the pine,
he whirrs the wind around him and finds the sweetness,
his rubies glint in the early spring sunlight
and the vibration of home reverberates
to the charm retuning to our valley,
early
but always always welcome.

⌘ As You Paint and I Write

I listen to you sing Joni Mitchell
in your studio while you paint,
hear the swish and splash of your paintbrush
dip-swirling and clinking in a glass,
the colors fading together in my mind,
hues blending into a moving sea,
and your sweet voice
your charmingly imperfect pitch
and tender hum
the clink of the brush
chime into the lines of this poem.

You don't even know I am listening so intently,
that your brushstrokes
are painting warmth onto my face
a smile on my lips,
     I could drink a case of you
I hum along as I write,
my chest fills with cerulean.

Your playlist of love songs
croons softly into my office,
makes it hard for me to focus on work
because my heart keeps getting pulled into
the songs and the space between us,
I rise in the chorus of one of our favorite lines,
turn and see you already silhouetted in my doorway,
your face gently tipped to touch the doorframe,
singing, we walk slowly to each other,
embrace in the endless songs that holds us,
the tenderness that sustains us.

We slow dance in the hallway,
all our colors fading together, a moving sea.

⌘ Growing into a Star *(for my mother, Estrelita)*

The more I grow into woman,
the more I become like you.

I think of your eyes,
almond-shaped brown beautiful,
soft welcoming globes
that see everything,
every
little
thing,
and though you may not *say* you see everything
I know you do, mom.

I think of your eyes
and I wonder what how many sunrises ascending
over fields of rice reflected gold on your young face,
Estrelita your parents named you— *little star*
mirroring the light above
and the light in the rice water below
and the bright glow of your own visions of a better life.
I think of your eyes
and how much they hold,
how they held my father's heart long enough
to bring your little girls into life,
to plant their tiny feet
on American soil so the golden rice fields of your past
became fields of golden opportunity stretched out before us,
and did you see that future all along?
Did you work and sweat and dream and cry
knowing that your little girls would someday fly?
I think of your eyes,
how they watch over every detail,
the depth,
the beauty,
the softness,

but mostly the laughter,
the way they crease at the edges from
a lifetime of smiles
given to strangers,
silly jokes told to friends,
tears of pride washing away all the pain,
your eyes speak volumes without a word,
they smile and laugh and sing
and remind us all of the joy that life can bring.
I think of your eyes
and I know right now they are seeing me.

I look in the mirror and see, I have your eyes.

The more I grow into woman,
the more I become like you.

I think of your hands,
the shape of their opening,
the long slender fingers,
long graceful nail beds,
red fingernails,
how hard your hands have worked
yet how they always look graceful,
building beauty all around us,
cleaning and cooking and praying,
covering us like wings of a mother bird.
Your hands have shaped me,
like clay I am formed in the reflection of you,
in this life, you hold us,
the daughters of your lineage,
a grandson now in the cradle of your care.

How much soil has passed through those fingers?
How many seeds were planted
by your green thumbs pushing through dirt?
How much care do your hands extend to
fruit-bearing trees, vegetables, flowers, herbs, grain,
the loving touch of our young faces,

the fingers combing our hair,
the clapping hands always cheering us on,
the holding and molding and shaping and scraping by
with almost nothing
but still open, your hands,
always willing to sacrifice, to give, so that we might live
a life of open hands.

In every picture taken of you,
you find a flower to touch,
a tree or a leaf to hang onto,
our running family joke is *"Hold the leaves!"*
but there is something much deeper,
there is a bond between a woman
and the universe,
there is a life force connection that transcends your body
and flows into the body of nature,
perhaps it is the jasmine
that wishes to hold the hand of a star,

perhaps it is the naked fig tree
wanting to dance with a Queen so she may bear a child,
perhaps the leaves don't want you to leave
saying *"hold my hand and don't let me go,"*
perhaps it is something that we may never know,
but there is magic in your hands,
there is light, and growth, and protection,
there are invisible flowers that grow from your fingertips
and you gift quiet rose petals to all you touch.

I look down at my fingers dancing across the keyboard
and see, I have your hands.

The more I grow into woman
the more I become like you.

I could list all of the ways in which
I am becoming more like you every day,
how I am proud to stand as a woman of strength and conviction,

how my heart is the way I move through the world,
how you wrote the beautiful poem of me
while I danced in your womb
and the echoes of those words
are finally forming from my mouth,
how I am also independent of you,
flying with my own wings,
my own dreams,
my own fierce and tender song,
but
there is a Golden Light reflecting a sunrise
climbing over distant rice fields,
becoming the brightest star shining in the night sky,
guiding my heart in everything I do.

That star is you, Mom.
That star is you.

⌘ Our America ***
(for Abrams, Warnock, and Ossoff)

It's a new day to wake up
in Our America—
it's the morning of January 6th
and all the peaches in Georgia
turned from orange
to blue,
blue plump in the trees,
blue blooming from grass roots,
blue knocking down all the red walls,
blue joining hands with every other color and saying US,
blue rising and flooding the streets
of this Southern state,
and the state of our country
is different today,
the scales have tipped
back on the side of Light,
and together in this America,
we have come back and won the fight,
and what do we do now as we wake in Our America?

We let our hearts fill with
the words of Reverend Raphael Warnock,
Georgia's first Black Senator
when he said—
"The other day, because this is America,
the 82-year-old- hands
that used to pick somebody else's cotton
went to the polls and picked
her youngest son
to be a United States Senator."

This is Our America,
where a Black woman named Stacey
Harriet Tubman-ed our nation back toward the stars

of freedom, and the underground houses
of Black voters stood up again
and again and again
though America is only starting
to stand up for them,
and when will we see
that Black Women have always been
the Real Mothers of this country,
have always waited in the wings to pull us
to their bosoms and say— *"come here, child, you gon' be alright."*

Today, America can see her wings,
and from under them we can all fly
side by side in gratitude
toward an un-resisted hope,
just think how far an arrow can shoot
that has been painfully pulled back for so long,
just feel the racehorses of our ideals
finally launching from the starting gates
we've been pushing against for years,
just think of how fast we can propel forward
when the hurdles and walls have all been cleared.

What will it feel like to not have to RESIST—
but to stand together with leaders
and hear our voices spill from their lips,
wanting to *build* instead of destroy,
wanting to *unite* instead of divide,
wanting to *fight* systemic racism
instead of fan its proud and ugly flames,
wanting to *protect* our planet
instead of deregulate its demise,
and I have to pause
and say, oh—
I haven't breathed this deep a sigh
in all of my life.

Of course, we have much work do to,
I am not naive,

but this is a day to mark all that we have achieved.
We have been through
the dark night of the soul of our country
and the sound of our voices rising since November
are drowning out the angry white noise of chaos,
the red hats will bury their heads in the sand
and across this broken and beautiful land
the stars on our flag will start to shine again,
the stripes that we have taken on our hearts
will turn to the stories of how we fought
and won in an uncivil war,
and going forward into tomorrow
I will still be compassion and empathy's soldier,
but this morning—
I write a poem for this moment,
I bow in words
to the Mover of Mountains Stacey Abrams,
to Senator Reverend Doctor Raphael Warnock
to Senator Jon Ossoff,
to President Joseph R. Biden,
to our first Black and South Asian Woman Vice President Kamala Harris.

It's a new day to wake up in Our America.

*** Later this same day, January 6th, 2021, just hours after I finished writing this poem, there was an armed and violent Insurrection at the United States Capitol, in Washington D.C.

⌘ My Whole Soul Is In It
(Inaugural Poem, for the Poets in the Resistance)

"To heal, we must remember."
    - The 46th President of the United States, Joseph R. Biden

It's already like a war story
in my mouth, making it to this moment,
the shrapnel embedded in our hearts still gleaming
with fresh wounds, and it is the morning
and trump is gone, riding still the tails
of his atrocities turned so-called wins,
tooting still his own sad little horn
even in the final moments
of his jilted departure,
"have a nice life"
he says, and you know what?
I will now,
we will now,
for it is morning,
it is *this* morning in America
we are awake and the sun is rising
after a four-year nightmare,
and we don't want to remember.

"To heal, we must remember."

We don't want to remember all that unfolded
during the demoralizing trump regime,
the times we cried and lost hope,
how we forgot to dream,
but we've written it all into poems, haven't we?
Took it upon our tender hearts to chronicle the chaos
like some weary scribes of human history,
like in the future some sentient beings will stumble
across our defiant light slivered in the darkness,
and say *here— there were poets with words*

holding evil to the fire.

To heal, I remember my own Catalog of American Carnage—
Grab them by the pussy, a poem,
the Muslim ban, a poem,
Paris Accord withdrawal, a poem,
un-shaping glaciers, I wrote a poem,
very good people on both sides, another poem,
children in cages, a poem and a foil blanket
worn like a cape, leading a protest,
transgender military ban, a poem,
North Korean nuclear face off, a poem,
the border wall, the hate, the nazis, poem poem poem,
school shootings and lockdown drills, poems,
another black boy dead,
another
another
another
another—
pandemic, poems, so many poems.
      I wouldn't write a poem for the insurrection,
      I wouldn't bend my words that low.

Every day, every lie, every new fresh hell,
the rancor and violence, the taste and the smell,
and I never went poem-numb from his callous (un)heart,
saw myself in the constant mode of fight or flight,
stomach tight, waiting for the next gut punch,
jaw grinding the names of the dead in my teeth,
and poetry was the only sword I had that felt right,
letters strung together to form a vibration of Light.

Love poems and nature poems too,
but naming his atrocities always bleeding through.

And it is morning now,
on the day of All Our Lords, January 20th, 2021,
and just for today, we can put down our swords,
the vacuous stain has been airlifted to *I don't really care where*,

and the sun is steadily rising over the reflection pool
shining over pillars of light that mark the 400,000 we've lost,
compassion and empathy made their first stop here last night,
the first act of this new administration touching down in Washington D.C.
was to remember our dead, to grieve and to reflect,
to remind us we are still whole in our humanness,
fragile in our loss,
stronger together in our hope,
and a Black COVID ICU nurse sang *Amazing Grace*
like an Angel,
and I wept at the beauty,
I wept for the return of our hearts,
the reflection of us in light shining into this morning,
this mourning, with a u, mourning with you,
the inverted mirror of backwards chaos upside-down everything
flipping back into the real, and a bird outside my window
is trumpeting a herald song, and it is morning,
and in America this morning, finally, I feel like I belong.
"To heal, we must remember"

Poets, we can look into our minds
and remember each line written into the library
of consciousness, scribbled in the dark
into the book of now,
our words running together
to form a criss-crossing network of the real peoples' history,
the true colors of our sorrow and joy,
and this morning I am ready
to burn it all into a new fire,
make it into a star
of *let's never get this close*
to destroying ourselves again.

I am ready to undocument the night
of its chaos, of its pain, I am ready
to write about hope and beauty again,
to fill all the white space with color,
stop the enjambments so we are all in line together,
walking toward a tomorrow where we are all on the same page.

Let this poem be my last reflection of that old country,
the inverted mirror we lost ourselves in
and found ourselves in again dressed as votes,
dressed as love and inextinguishable hope,
and this morning, a new chapter of our story begins,
we wake up with shattered ceilings under our feet
the glass on the ground and in our hair
shimmering like the cosmos fell,
it will be soft, not sharp,
it will sing and hum in the song of becoming sky,
and today in America
a Black South Asian Woman
(all of us women) will RISE.

I am an American flag
on that distant Inaugural lawn,
my stars and stripes waving
like a prayer and a poem in the winds of change
my colors of reclaimed red, white, and blue
shine with new and vibrant hues,
and this is my country again, my God,
this is our country again.

On this hard fought Inauguration Day,
after I sing and cry and dance distant with all of you,
after the reality of change sinks into my bones,
and my tears of hope wash my spirit new,
I will roll up my sleeves, America—
we have work to do

and my whole Soul is in it.

⌘ Decrescendo*

41 feels so different,
like I have settled into my hips a little,
widened the pelvic floor of my heart
and let in the light of strangers,
tendered the flames of virtual squares
with hands outstretched
and promises of a world that is better than this,
emerging from this human cocooning we've endured,
how much another perspective can say,
angles of sight lip-synching life lines
into a fallen star across an ocean,
and so many things are dying.

So many things are still dying.

I can't stop buying plants,
never really had an interest before,
but now I'm crowding every slant of light
in our dark house
with armies of green to battle a loss I can't name.
My office windows crammed with peace lily, orchid, ferns,
ficus, philodendron, and strange little succulents,
one called *baby toes*, another *baby necklace*,
another that looks like dragon teeth,
the sharp and the soft together in a shallow pot,
a new friend on my desk is called a prayer plant, *goeppertia lancifolia*,
violet and green it folds up its hands every night and opens in the morning,
joints and hinges of stems speaking in quiet unfolding genus,
and I pray in poems beside it just wanting to make things live around me.

I hate to admit this but a hummingbird died in our greenhouse,
once she flew in, she couldn't figure out how to fly down and out the open door,
something about the way a hummingbird's hover doesn't let them fly down
when they are scared, only up, only skyward to blue.
I found her caught in the plastic winterizing liner on the inside roof,

her iridescent body was tiny in my hands,
I held her in my palm and moved her in the sunlight,
warming her as her tiny soul left, feathers still glinting in the light,
this small stillness in my fingers was like nothing I've ever felt,
her vibration hum and whirr silenced and still,
and it's like the whole world stopped for me, again,
holding a totem of spirit with my mundane flesh,
my warmth and her finite light ended here in my hands,
I hate to admit this but I can't let her go.

In Buenos Aires, a dear friend in her 80's just told us she has covid.
I can hear her heavy thick accent, her curiosity, her laughter,
we speak Spanish to each other in a way that makes me feel close,
she dances, even up to now, even through cancer
and breaking her middle finger and wearing a cast
that gives a fuck you to the world, she laughs and she dances
and stays angry at the government in Argentina,
and I want to dance with her, say *baila conmigo, corazón*,
tell her to lean on me, hold her arm under the elbow, I remember years ago
her grandchildren were swept away in a tsunami in Chile,
clutched in the mouth of an unfair god,
and it seems that same god is hungry,
and I can't let her go, I can't let her go,
want to send her a hummingbird on the winds of vitality,
alive and shining,
want to water my prayers into all of these plants,
so that everything lives,
but I whisper in Spanish to a soul becoming a rainbow—

querida hermana del cielo,
no hay ninguna persona quien puede resistir su ascensión,
levántate, amiga de las estrellas,
todos los colores son tuyos,
y te amo, te amo siempre, Beatriz.

The praying hands of the lancifolia fold at her name,
at so many names.

I have settled into 41, the apex of sunrising

beginning a long decrescendo of learning
the lesson I never wanted to know—

how to let go.

* Rest in Pachamama, Beatriz. Te amo siempre.

⌘ Harbingers of This Particular Spring

Did you ever notice how daffodils are like little trumpets?
Swords of green stab their way up
through cold earth and crunchy leaves,
blooms of bright yellow
open like a thousand little sunrises
reminding us of the taste of hope,
toot toot too too they call like a birdsong of flowers,
and we know that soon the world will open up again *green*,
that this drab cold naked grey sky
will fill again with life and song and fruit and flight,
the daffodil laughs at how we cling to such things as seasons,
as reasons to push through with hope in our hearts,
yet we do, *hope*,
yet we do, *cling*,
because this particular spring
means a little more than the springs before,
it's as if we've fought the darkest winter of our lifetimes,
like we are backpedalling from the precipice of a cliff-edge year,
like we survived on the balm of our own souls and collective fear,
our leaves and petals in our solitary soil,
the social distance of our individual birdsongs,
the untouchable skin of our peach-ripened hearts,
and it is not just the cold winter under our feet today,
but half a million of our dearly departed
buried like seeds that will never bloom again,
or scattered to the wind like the fallen leaves of this painful winter,
and I admit, this poem started as a sunrising daffodil,
the harbinger of hope and healing,
but I cannot help but feel the call to mourning,
mourning,
maybe just one more time before we let the sun rise,
remember,
remember what we went through together,
remember how we still found ways to touch,
look what we are almost on the other side of,

look behind at the year in our collective rearview mirror,
and take time to reflect,
be humble and thankful,
be silent and still,
yes, all is blooming,
the harbingers of spring
are standing ready on their highest pedestals,
the chorus of frogs will sing the night songs to awaken blades of grass,
the tulip magnolias and redbuds bursting with their violet blooms
will quell the violence on the streets and the elephants in the room, observe
and listen, even closer that ever before,
let this spring heal you,
let the wash of neon green fill in the aching parts of you,
see the naked tree of your empty hands
filling again with all that was leaving you last year,
family, friends, grandchildren, lovers,
the leaving becoming new leaves filling you again,
bursting from bud into bright blue sky,
ancient and new,
perennial,
it's not just the frogs and flowers returning,
not just the nesting birds fledgling their way into flight,
not just the newly planted vegetable seeds singing possibility to the empty tables,
but the harbingers are heralding the cusp of our lives returning,
the world we once knew equinoxing
into something we have yet to behold,
the story of a *new humanity* yet to unfold,
where we take our lessons on survival and growing forward with us,
our appreciation for family and community,
our children's resilience and strength,
our standing up together against all forms of hate,
our reminders that love is never too late,
we take our powerful votes and our joined voices,
our reverence for the natural world and our better choices,
we take all the lessons that have helped us make it to this other side,
and together
we turn our faces toward the sun
and let in all the Light.

⌘ About the Author

about her: beacon persistent
manifestor of previously uncrossed stars
puller down of such cosmos

voice of the voiceless
undaunted historian of human striving
protest sign in poems held up against systems
breaker of systems

the poet is the breaker of systems
the poet is the builder of new systems, worlds

perhaps she is from those other worlds, here, in fact,
on sabbatical from stint as stardust
walking in human feet
for a cycle of orbits that has no language here

life on earth is a practice in darkness
overcoming
the poet speaks the language of overcoming

she is, too,

wife of master naturalist so de facto master naturalist
leaf inspector, bloom herald, bird singer
onto page
holder of light against all things
seemingly heretofore
opaque

⌘ A Poem You Write, Dear Reader

Take this space for yourself. Grab a pen. Mine the stardust that remains etched in your cells after what we all experienced together. Write. Reflect. Put your feelings down onto the page. How did you break? How did you grow? What do you take with you into tomorrow?

ACKNOWLEDGMENTS

The author would like to thank the editors and staff of the following publications, literary journals, and anthologies in which versions of these poems have previously appeared.

As The World Burns Anthology: "Smiling With My Eyes" and "Unbouyant"

Bellevue Literary Review: "Fertile" and "Brighter When Wet"

Boundless 2021 Anthology: "I Find My 2020 Glasses from New Years," "My Whole Soul Is In It," and "About the Author"

Cutthroat, A Journal of the Arts: "Essence"

The Elpis Pages: "Izibongo for Black Women"

Idle Class Magazine: "What Stitches Us Together"

Lavender Review: "A Baptism Reflecting the Celestial"

Madness Muse Press: "Not Enough Words for Light," "Makeshift Memorial," "Plume," "Microcosm Macrochoas," and "The Language of Hitting Bottom"

NELLE: "Water for Martians"

POETRY Magazine: "Filling Spice Jars As Your Wife"

Rise Up Review: "Palette"

Rough Cut Press: "This America, How Much More Can We Take?"

Solstice Literary Magazine: "Planting Seeds and Tasting Flowers During the End of Days"

SWWIM: "Ring Sing"

TAB: The Journal of Poetry & Poetics: "Into Wildflower Into Field" and "Tendrils"

West Trestle Review: "Today I Washed My Hands in a Mucky Koi Pond"

Whale Road Review: "Lazarus"

Yellow Chair Review: "Temple Dogs 石 獅 賦"

MY GRATITUDE

Honestly, I am thankful to you first, dear reader. Thank you for going into this journey with me in poems, and for all the vibrations that your mind and heart sent out as you read and recounted this unprecedented time, counted the dead, counted the hopes, and counted the stars that surround your own life with light. As I write these notes of gratitude, we are still very much in the midst of another round of the pandemic, the tunnel brighter for a moment, but pulling us back into the dark for more lessons we need to learn about how to love one another on this planet. Thank you for being one who feels alongside me that beauty and goodness will still somehow triumph. Stay safe.

Thank you to all who have been on my poetry dream team thus far, each reader and supporter a star in this constellation— my mother Ester and sister Diana, cornerstones; my inner circle; my fellow poets out there writing the world right in your poems; all the editors of lit mags who believed in these words before they became this book; my WNP family locally and virtually across the globe, the 3,000+ poets who touched my hand through the screen each week. We hold each other up. Thank you to Del Greer, my eagle-eyed copyeditor. Thank you Margo McGehee-Kelly, MamaD, and Gin Hartnett for your unwavering support and love. Thank you to Jane Hirshfield, Julie E. Bloemeke, and Crystal C. Mercer for your Magic. Thank you Amanda and Liam Lezra for your sweetness. Thank you to every woman I call "Sis" and every man I call 'Brother," you are my tribe of fellow warriors, fellow servers of humanity. I see you. Stay strong.

A huge, heartfelt thank you to the absolutely humbling cast of advanced readers who wrote the most generous blurbs a poet could ask for— Ellen Bass, Naomi Shihab Nye, Juan Felipe Herrera, Richard Blanco, Minnie-Bruce Pratt, Melissa Studdard, JP Howard, Danusha Laméris, Mary Meriam, and James Crews. Thank you and big big love to my FlowerSong Press publisher Edward Vidaurre for believing in the stardust of this book, for working with me hand in hand to make it shine, and for your commitment to amplifying voices of color like mine.

Thank you to all the essential workers who are still fighting the battles on the front lines of this pandemic every day— doctors, nurses, EMTs, hospital workers, teachers (a huge bow of thanks to teachers), grocery workers, postal workers, moms, dads, therapists, everyone helping another person keep going another day. I bang my pots and pans on the balcony of my heart for you.

Thank you to the stars, to the cosmos, to the fireflies, to the birds and bees, to the whole natural world trying to survive us.

Finally, my deepest gratitude goes to my wife and love of my life, Joann— the only person in the world I would want to spent the apocalypse with, the Pi in the sky dreamer, the one who lifted all my veils, the one who inspires me, the one who nurtures me, the one who brings the wild beauty and peace of mother earth to my lips to drink daily, the one who pushes my spirit to keep striving for my truest and highest Self. Normally, Joann paints the covers for my books, but now I can say the only ones who have painted my books are Joann and the blooming star-bursting Universe itself. Seems fitting. Joann, I love you infinitely, darling one.

Oh, hi again. Still here? Did you write your own stardust pandemic reflection poem, dear reader? Do you want to share it with me? Snap a pic and email it to kaicoggin@gmail.com, or post it on social media and use the hashtag #MiningForStardust. Let's form a constellation.

ABOUT KAI

Kai Coggin is the author of *MINING FOR STARDUST* (FlowerSong Press 2021), *INCANDESCENT* (Sibling Rivalry Press 2019), *WINGSPAN* (Golden Dragonfly Press 2016), and *PERISCOPE HEART* (Swimming with Elephants Publications 2014), as well as a spoken word album *SILHOUETTE* (2017). She is a queer woman of color who thinks Black Lives Matter, and a Teaching Artist in poetry with the Arkansas Arts Council and Arkansas Learning Through the Arts, specializing in bringing poetry and creative writing to roughly 3,500 students each school year, in residencies statewide. Coggin also hosts of the longest running consecutive weekly open mic series in the country—Wednesday Night Poetry, which has never missed a week since February 1, 1989. Ever.

Recently awarded the 2021 Governor's Arts Award and named "Best Poet in Arkansas" by the Arkansas Times, her fierce and powerful poetry has been nominated four times for The Pushcart Prize, as well as Bettering American Poetry 2015, and Best of the Net 2016 and 2018. Her poems have appeared or are forthcoming in *POETRY*, *Cultural Weekly*, *Solstice Literary Magazine*, *Bellevue Literary Review*, *Entropy*, *SWWIM*, *Sinister Wisdom*, *Lavender Review*, *Luna Luna*, *Halfway Down the Stairs*, *Blue Heron Review*, *Tupelo Press*, *West Trestle Review*, and elsewhere. Coggin is Associate Editor at *The Rise Up Review*. She lives with her wife and their two adorable dogs, Genghis and Layla, in the valley of a small mountain in Hot Springs National Park, Arkansas.

www.kaicoggin.com

To invite Kai to zoom into your classroom, or to read in-person at your literary festival, LGBTQ event, school, university, bookclub, or library— please contact FlowerSong Press or reach out to her at kaicoggin@gmail.com.

Facebook: Kai Coggin
Twitter: @skailight
IG: @skailight

Stay safe and well. Keep mining for stardust, bright ones.